Champagne Ru

The golden age of French ru

The famous 1951 French tourists
Back: J. Audoubert, M. Lopez, G. Calixte, E. Brousse, G. Delaye,
R. Perez, A. Beraud, E. Ponsinet, O. Lespes; middle: P. Bartoletti,
J. Duhau (coach), R. Duffort, R. Contrastin, L. Mazon, V. Cantoni,
A. Blain (manager), A. Puig-Aubert, M. Andre, G. Genoud,
F. Montrucolis, F. Rinaldi, R. Samatan (coach); front: M. Martin,
J. Merquey, M. Bellan, R. Caillou, J. Dop, J. Crespo, G. Comes.

Henri Garcia

Translation and statistics by Roger Grime

London League Publications Ltd

Champagne Rugby
The golden age of French rugby league

© Copyright Henri Garcia; this translation © Roger Grime. Foreword © Reg Gasnier

The moral right of Henri Garcia to be identified as the author and Roger Grime as the translator have been asserted.

Cover design © Stephen McCarthy. Photographs © the photographer or contributor of the photograph. No copyright has been intentionally infringed.

Front cover photo: Raymond Contrastin in action in 1951. (Courtesy Louis Bonnery) Back cover photo: Puig Aubert after the 1951 third test triumph. (Courtesy Bernard Pratviel)

A CIP catalogue record for this book is available from the British Library.

Originally published in France in 1961 by La Table Ronde.

First published in Great Britain in September 2007 by:
London League Publications Ltd, P.O. Box 10441, London E14 8WR

ISBN: 978-1903659-34-2

Cover design by: Stephen McCarthy Graphic Design
                    46, Clarence Road, London N15 5BB

Layout: Peter Lush

Printed and bound by: Biddles Ltd
                       King's Lynn, Great Britain

Dedicated to the Tricolors and Treizistes everywhere

Foreword

When asked to write a foreword to a book which chronicles the history of the first French teams to tour Australasia, I was delighted.

We could certainly do with a strong Tricolor side to once again grace our shores and thrill full stadia everywhere. A viable fourth team is a 'must' if international rugby league is to regain its lustre on the world stage.

That 1951 side was an absolute joy to watch. Though small by today's standards, they ran the Australians ragged all around the Sydney Cricket Ground and Lang Park. I was a young lad at school then and marvelled at the kicking prowess of the great Puig-Aubert.

Touring teams came and went, but my eagerness to have a crack at the French just grew. Finally, I was selected in the 1957 President's Cup team to play in the centres alongside Johnny Riley, who later went on to represent the Kangaroos on the 1959 tour of England and France. That President's Cup side eventually went on to win the Premiership and included future first-graders Kenny Anderson, Johnny Stathers and the reliable winger, Brian Messiter.

I had the honour of playing 36 tests and three World Cup games for Australia, but always got an extra thrill playing against the French. In my time, so many fine players pulled on the Tricolor jersey and while some who spring to mind may have lacked size, they more than made up for it with toughness and determination. Any Aussie victory was certainly hard-earned, and the French ability to play dry weather football in the wettest conditions was simply uncanny.

On one tour, I recall Peter Gallagher throwing his arms up in sheer desperation as he vainly chased French shadows and, I must admit, their infuriating changes of direction frustrated all of us.

I vividly remember the big fella up front, Marcel Bescos, and his back-row colleague, the powerful Jean Barthe. Now they were a handful! Our opposite numbers, the world-class Antoine Jiminez and Gilbert Benausse, certainly kept us very busy trying to contain them. They were fast, elusive and superb readers of a game.

Unfortunately, the fabulous Puig-Aubert only toured in 1951, but he was succeeded by another tremendous goalkicker in Pierre Lacaze and many were the torrid clashes we enjoyed over the years.

Sure, international sport is intense on the playing fields of the world, but one of my fondest memories came off the pitch. Harry Wells and I had the great pleasure of having dinner at the home of the 1951 front-rower, Lolo Mazon. His wife and daughter had limited English and Harry's French was non-existent. Thank God for my schoolboy French and somehow we all got through with lasting memories, and appreciation, of some exceptional French home cooking. I still cherish the ashtray I was given for, while I don't smoke, it stands there to remind me of the great friendships rugby league propagates.

As I said earlier, the game has certainly changed. Little blokes have given way to centres of 15 stones or more running round as fast as we ever did. Regardless of how it's played, I would love to see a strong French presence once more to keep the Kiwis, Pommies and our own representative sides honest in international rugby league.

I always enjoyed my time touring France and hosting their teams over here. I was known to translate the French team calls on the field and try and get our guys in position which always gave my French friends some grief! My name, Gasnier, has roots in France and they always joked that I had a place in the French team whenever I wanted.

As you can see, French rugby league will always have a cherished place among my memories. Bonne chance!

Reg Gasnier AM,
Australian Kangaroo tour and test captain.

Reg Gasnier was Australia's youngest ever test captain. He played for St George from 1959 to 1967, scoring 127 tries in 129 games, at a time when St George dominated the game in Australia. He also played 16 times for New South Wales, scoring 13 tries. For Australia, he scored 26 tries in 36 test appearances, and played three games in the 1960 World Cup. He is one of the greatest Australian players of the post-war era.

Photo: Reg Gasnier in action.

Translator's note

Most of the English-speaking world has not, up until now, had the opportunity of reading Henri Garcia's consummate account of the first three French tours down under. It is fascinating to appreciate those glorious days from a Gallic perspective and enjoy, for example, the often differing standpoints taken on the same incidents.

In my opinion, Henri Garcia's book serves as a reference point for the 'Golden Age' of French rugby league. As with any translation, it is practically impossible to convey every nuance and colloquialism. I have aimed to preserve the contemporary feel and tried to avoid being stilted, but if I have failed, especially in the early sections, please forgive me.

The rugby league family world-wide has gone out of its way to help, for which I would like to thank everyone who has contributed, by providing photos, research for missing statistics and records and in many other ways. These people include: in New Zealand: John Coffey, Don Hammond, Bernie Wood, Bud Lisle, Peter Kerridge, Bill Whitehead and Karen Wickliffe; in Australia: Sean Fagan, Peter and Reg Gasnier and my old friend from Brisbane, Bill Abernethy; in the UK: Ray French, Ray Gent, Harry Edgar, Mike Rylance, Tim Butcher, Dave Hadfield and Denis Whittle; in France: Denis Tillinac of the original publishers La Table Ronde, Bernard Pratviel, Laurent Roldos, John Chapman and especially Louis Bonnery who has been so generous with his time and use of material. Above all, I must thank Henri Garcia and Carole, his daughter, who have been such enthusiastic and diligent allies. and in particular, Alex Service, for his priceless mastery of technology.

I would also like to thank those who contributed to the production of the book: Peter Lush and Dave Farrar from London League Publications Ltd, Michael O'Hare for sub-editing, Steve McCarthy for designing the cover, Robert Gate and Alex Service for help with photographs and the staff at Biddles Ltd for the printing.

Special thanks go to my wife, Ann, for her help with the text and for indulging me in this project.

All my proceeds from the book will go towards a memorial to the Tricolors, hopefully at the Sydney Cricket Ground, where so many fans saw so much thrilling history made.

If I have managed to convey even a little of the Tricolors' passion and pride, I will be satisfied. If I have helped you appreciate Henri's affectionate and entertaining masterpiece, I will be delighted.

Roger Grime

Henri Garcia shows Roger Grime Gilbert Benausse's last test jersey.
(Courtesy Roger Grime)

England versus France 1939 at St Helens:
The French team which defeated England for the first time.
Antoine Blain is third from the left in the back row, Max Rousié
is with the ball in the front row. (Courtesy Louis Bonnery)

Preface

The Golden Years

It's taken more than a century of crises, disagreements, conflicts and equivocation for the Rugby Football Union to accept, and finally embrace, the evil of professionalism. After all, "Evil be to him who evil thinks" is the nicely turned phrase which has become the motto of the British Crown. What a pity that the learned officials of rugby's Victorian era didn't follow the example of the Northerners who, by pursuing a more pragmatic path, created a more modern version of the game.

In the same vein, union's harsh treatment of rugby across the Channel in France allowed league to prosper for, in 1934, Britain and Australia seized the opportunity offered by the rift between the British Empire and the French Republic to promote the "new" rugby. What we in France call the war between XV and XIII, to simplify the titles of the two codes, went so well in the Treizistes' favour, that Union was thought to have been all but wiped out. The Second World War, however, staunched union's mortal haemorrhage, when, under the cloak of the German occupation, a real abuse of authority took place.

Concerned about the nation's moral health, the famous Wimbledon tennis champion, Jean Borotra, who had been appointed Minister for Sport in Marshal Petain's government, decided that from 8 September 1940, all professional sections, in particular rugby league, would be banned. But union sympathisers, who held influential posts in the Vichy collaborationist regime, stooped to even more contemptible depths. A former Perpignan and France fly-half, Jep Pascot, who had succeeded Jean Borotra, issued a decree, signed by Philippe Petain, which, on 19 December 1940, dissolved the French Rugby League and confiscated all its assets. Liberation Day dawned on 16 September 1944, but not for rugby league. Frantic lobbying by "right-minded" men in power blocked it, and forced the French Rugby League to drop from its title the word "rugby", which was judged to be the sole prerogative of union. It was as late as 13 July 1947, that it was finally admitted to the National Sports' Committee, but only as "The 13-a-side game". Despite all this, the memory of those glorious years, 1934 to 1940, led a host of clubs to join the Federation which organised an elite structure based on the big cities: Paris, Lyons, Marseilles, Toulouse and Bordeaux, but at the same time reclaimed its traditional strongholds of Perpignan, Carcassonne, Villeneuve, Avignon, Albi and Bayonne.

I cannot remember a more brilliant generation than that which sprang up when rugby league was reborn. There were stars like Puig-Aubert, Elie Brousse, Edouard Ponsinet, Jo Crespo, Vincent Cantoni, Jean Dop, Raymond Contrastin, Gaston Comes, Jackie Merquey, Gilbert Benausse and so many more. Then, rugby league was more popular than union.

In 1949, I was a young journalist, starting out on the sports daily, *L'Equipe*, and I had the opportunity to live through this 'Golden Age'. Even better, at a time when rugby union big-wigs sidelined the press with contempt and condescension, I found friendship and support in rugby league circles. I have fond memories of the warm welcome I received as a reporter from the officials of Wigan, Bradford, St Helens and Leeds, among others, but especially from the great Bill Fallowfield, secretary of the RFL. Similarly, I remember all those happy times on extended tours of Australia and New Zealand, thanks to the friendship of famous players like Clive Churchill, Johnny Raper, Reg Gasnier, to name but a few, and the respect shown to me by officials of the calibre of Jersey Flegg and Ron McGregor.

The famous first tour of 1951, when we disembarked in Marseilles after a month-long voyage home, culminated in driving in procession up the famous Canebière, with crowds in excess of 100,000 turning it into a Roman triumph. In 1954, the youngest-ever President of the Federation, Paul Barrière, was the driving force behind the inaugural World Cup in which Britain beat France in the final at Parc des Princes, Paris. It was 1987 before rugby union caught up.

Sadly, rugby league in France failed to put in place a framework to profit from its popularity. Stars faded, but new ones failed to take their place. The arrival of professionalism stretched rugby union's advantage. Nevertheless, memories of the epic post-war Treiziste era have remained vivid, the years when the Australians coined the well-deserved epithet, "champagne rugby".

I would like to take this opportunity of thanking Roger Grime for his interest in a book I brought out back in 1961. I am grateful for his remarkable commitment to reminding us of the glorious past. Thanks to him, that 'golden age', when the Cockerels of the 1950s showed they were no ordinary birds, is alive again.

Henri Garcia

Contents

The pen pictures in this edition were not part of the original book, but were written by Roger Grime based on material used at the time.

It was difficult to obtain photographs for this book, and some are not as high a quality as we would usually use. This is not a reflection on any photographer or contributor of a photograph.

Left:
The great French pre-war star Max Rousié in action in 1935 for Villeneuve.

Below:
Jean Galia, a key figure in the early days of French rugby league. (Courtesy Robert Gate)

North versus south

Sometimes, it's almost as if the force of nature drives a pupil to become his teacher's most dangerous rival. So it was that France set out for Australia to conquer the 'Masters', the Kangaroos, who had been prime movers in the birth of French rugby league. First, however, let's look back over the strange story of the great rugby schism.

Rugby football, with rules codified at Rugby School, had conquered the whole of the British Isles with its traditional form of manly sport which harked back to that older football, whose violence had led the Kings of England to ban it over centuries. Yet, at the very time that the sport was taking a real hold on society across the Channel, the Industrial Revolution was transforming the old England. The savage beauty of the north, beloved of Emily and Charlotte Bronte, was sadly eaten away by a gigantic cancer of factories. Only its 'Wuthering Heights', too poor and desolate, were left unsullied by the century's 'dark satanic mills'.

Everywhere else, the gentle English countryside was abandoned for high wages in Eldorados under sooty skies. Liverpool, Manchester, Leeds, Bradford, Huddersfield and Hull expanded to the point where they seemed to form a colossal metropolis. The working man appeared to have been forgotten in the chaos but he was there, carrying an enormous burden which soon became too heavy to bear. Strikes broke out all over the place for work to stop at midday on Saturdays, which was how the workers of the North, in a world's first, won what we can call 'The English week'.

A free Saturday afternoon in our Midi is great for teasing trout or a petanque match, but Yorkshire, Lancashire and Cumberland were enclaves of boredom where the pubs traditionally stayed closed till 5pm. What was there to do while a wife was busy with the ritual of preparing for another day of mourning that was a northern Sunday? Response was swift. A northerner only had one thing to occupy him from 1pm to 6pm on a Saturday afternoon: sport in general and rugby in particular.

If he was young and fit, he pulled on his boots, but if the passage of time and whisky had taken their toll, he'd happily plonk himself on a touchline and show his commitment by occasionally bellowing, "Come on, lads!" or right at the crucial moment, "Go on, forwards!" On winter Saturday afternoons at the end of the century, your average Englishman wouldn't have succumbed to the warmth of the fireside any more than today. Bigger and bigger crowds were packing football grounds and with the English being, as everyone knows, shrewd businessmen, very soon the turnstile was introduced at which the sportsman preferred to cough up his two or three shillings rather than stop at home. Since the subjects of Her Gracious Majesty were no fools, the players, who guaranteed cash at the gate, demanded certain perks. As these could not be refused, the north of England saw the birth of professional football towards the end of the nineteenth century. Posh London society cried scandal and established the dividing line between association football, or soccer, and rugby football as follows: "Football is a game for gentlemen played by hooligans whereas rugby is a game for hooligans played by gentlemen".

Money wasn't a motive for gentlemen rugby players – they weren't short of it! Workers, on the other hand, in the mines and factories of the north, didn't see anything wrong at all in making up lost wages by drawing a full week from employers who were kind enough not to dock hours lost to rugby. This practice, which today shocks no-one, provoked a right rumpus at the Rugby Union towards the end of the century. A real battle of Hernani* ensued between the progressives of the industrial North and the conservative southern gentry especially those from London, Oxford and Cambridge.

The northern counties - Yorkshire, Lancashire, Cumberland and Cheshire - didn't take at all kindly to the London-based leadership of the Rugby Union, who treated them as poor relations despite their having won the inter-county championship regularly since its inception. The Northerners thought they weren't well enough represented at the top and that their best players, mostly ordinary working men, were being overlooked in favour of chaps from Oxford and Cambridge Universities, who viewed them with contempt.

When northerners asked for lost wages to be taken into account, southerners indignantly objected. After a stormy vote denied them justice, the Northerners quit the Rugby Union. On 29 August 1895, at the George Hotel in Huddersfield, the Northern Rugby Football Union was founded, which, in 1922, became the Rugby Football League. Free of London control, the northern clubs launched massive reforms with leading players awarded six shillings per match day, provided they stayed in full-time employment. The most spectacular rule change was undoubtedly the reduction in the number of players. Only a few years earlier, in 1877, the Rugby Union had adopted a reduction to 15 from the 20 imposed by the Universities in 1873. Thanks to better and better training, players

*Hernani: A play by Victor Hugo whose opening night was marred by brawling cliques.

had shown such physical improvement that this change was inevitable. In the beginning, rugby was played school against school, but there was much confusion which was why the numbers were soon universally limited to 15.

For the northerners to go further and cut out the wing forwards was simple progress and the legislators of the Rugby Union would doubtless have brought in the same reform themselves, if the dissidents up north hadn't beaten them to it. A new form of rugby had been born, a less complex game which wanted to prune away all its older relation's dead wood. Less complicated and more athletic, it demanded greater speed, vitality and toughness while affording much less recovery time. And so began the feud between the two rugbys, a kind of minor war of religion in which latent antagonism between orthodox and reformed sometimes led to open warfare.

1933: England versus Australia

Above: Action from the first rugby league match in France. Australia beat England 63-13 in front of 10,000 fans on a freezing cold day. Dave Brown scored 27 points for the Australians, with 3 tries and 9 goals. (Photo: Courtesy Henri Garcia)

Left: The match programme.

1934: A tour to England and the first international

The French team that faced England in Paris on 15 April 1934. Jean Galia is holding the ball (Courtesy Louis Bonnery)

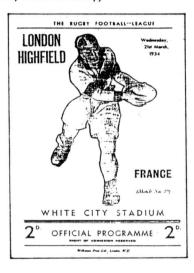

Programmes from two of the matches on the 1934 French tour to England. The French team won 26-23 at Hull, but lost the other five games.

The Warrington programme gave the French team "a most hearty welcome" and recalled how the English and French had fought side by side in the Great War, and now in a time of peace could play together.
(Courtesy Warrington Wolves RLFC)

Gaston Comes in action against Australia in 1949.
(Courtesy Louis Bonnery)

Jean Galia: revolutionary

The British have always found French rugby guilty of something. True, it has sometimes ignored convention and its misdeeds have twice led to suspensions, in 1913 and 1931. After 'Perfidious Albion' cast the FFR (French Rugby Union) into the wilderness, the RFL thought the time was ripe for a missionary expedition. What clinched it was the arrival in England of the Kangaroos in the autumn of 1933.

Harry Sunderland, the tour manager, was very keen on expansion, so on the morning of 3 October 1933, the following left for Paris: Harry Sunderland, the Scot John Wilson (secretary of the RFL) and three notables, Joe Lewthwaite, Walter Popplewell and Wilf Gabbat, all future RFL presidents. It was unthinkable to make contact with the officials of the FFR so they spied out the land by the back door. John Wilson, who had represented Great Britain at cycling in the 1912 Stockholm Olympics, thought the best way was to contact someone well versed in French sport - his friend Victor Breyer, a member of the International Cyclists' Union and editor of *Echo des Sports*. Wilson and Sunderland reached agreement with Breyer to stage an exhibition match between England and Australia at the Stade Pershing, on 31 December 1933.

So that they could make contact with key figures in French rugby, Victor Breyer advised the emissaries from across the Channel to meet up with a young journalist who covered rugby for *Sporting* and who was none other than the sadly missed Maurice Blein.

The RFL officials wanted to invite a group of French players to come to England and try out the new game. Maurice Blein's view was that they mustn't put in charge any official who had broken away from the FFR, but there was, at the same time, a player, Jean Galia, who would make a bold leader.

Jean Galia was one of the leading lights of French rugby whom the English had voted the best forward in Europe. Great player and shrewd businessman he may have been, but in that October 1933, he was an angry man. The Federation had just suspended him over some mysterious affair. After signing a contract with Quillan worth 80,000 francs with the Federation raising no objection at all, Jean Galia later moved on to Villeneuve, followed by the three Catalan stars, Bardes, Noguères and Serre-Martin. That really caused ripples in the Federation pond and several frogs croaked scandal. Their bloodhounds were unleashed on the trail and a postal worker from Villeneuve was bribed to divert all mail containing evidence that the three Catalans weren't just going to the capital of prunes for plums.

One day, the spy intercepted a telegram addressed to Noguères in which there was mention of "travelling expenses", signed "Jean". Just like claiming your dog's got rabies so you can kill it, the Federation wallahs, who didn't like Jean Galia's strong personality one little bit, declared that this Jean was Jean Galia. Even though he'd sworn in front of a Federation inquiry, and continued to maintain all his life that he had not sent the telegram, he was suspended.

From that day on, he was after revenge. When the RFL delegation got in touch, he agreed to attend the Australia versus England match in Paris on 31 December 1933. That New Year's Eve might have been freezing cold, but 20,000 spectators still packed the Stade Pershing. Despite the icy pitch, the exhibition was a resounding success with Australia winning 63-13 and the speed of the game astonishing the French crowd. At the final whistle, John Wilson and Harry Sunderland met up with Jean Galia who just said, "When do you want a French team to play in England?"

The tour was arranged for spring 1934, and such was Jean Galia's prestige, he had no problem in finding 16 leading players to go with him and experience the "new rugby". The 17 pioneers who set out on their adventure at the beginning of March were:

Galia (C.A. Villeneuve), Recaborde (Section Paloise), Duhau (S.A. Bordelais), Samatan (S.U. Agen), Carrère (R.C. Narbonne), Porra (Lyon O.U.), Blanc (Capbreton), Petit (S.L. Nancy), Mathon (Oyonnax), Lambert (Avignon), Barbazanges (Roanne), Nouel (S.A. Bordelais), Cassagneau (Esperaza), Amila (Lezignan), Vignals (Toulouse), Dechavanne (Roanne) and Fabre (Lezignan).

Galia's Boys lost 30-27 to Wigan on 6 March, the following day to London Highfield at White City and again to Leeds on 14 March. The first representative game, against the RFL Selection, took place at Warrington on 17 March and ended in another defeat, 32-16. Although it was short, the tour exhausted the French who found the rugby super-fast. The fifth match, at Hull on 24 March, brought Galia's Boys their first win by 26-23 but we can't take eternal glory from it because, with only 12 fit men, they brought in a 'ringer' from Bramley. Under the name of Eugène Vignial, he was the architect of the victory! Finally, the learning curve ended with a heavy defeat, 35-13 at Salford, on 26 March 1934.

Although the results weren't all that brilliant, something good did come out of the tour. With relations broken off between the FFR and the Rugby Football Union, the introduction of rugby league gave the French public the opportunity of once more watching international matches.

As far back as 6 April, the Ligue Française de Rugby à XIII had deposited its Articles of Association with the prefect of Police in Paris. It was strange that the first president, François Cadoret, deputy mayor of Riec-Sur-Belon, should come from Brittany, not one of rugby's hot-beds, while the other members were: Messrs. Vinson, Galia, Bordeneuve, Machavoine, Meunier, Delblat, Bernat and Maurice Blein.

Straight away, the Ligue arranged a game with England for 15 April at Stade Buffalo, which turned out to be an enormous success with hundreds locked out of a packed stadium. The FFR, predictably, sent a few trouble-makers to cause disruption, but they were nearly lynched by the crowd.

Plenty of players fancied this new game and followed in the footsteps of Jean Galia and his pioneers. With hundreds of new members, the Ligue wanted to strike while the iron was hot and so asked England to send over the powerful Yorkshire County team.

The itinerary saw the Englishmen on 5 May at Stade Buffalo, the 6th at Villeneuve, the 10th at Bordeaux and the 13th at Pau. The tour had actually started earlier, on 1 May in Lyons, where Maurice Tardy, a humble ball-bearing salesman, had been bitten by two bugs: rugby and promoting. Although the ball-bearings have since rolled so nicely for our friend Maurice that he is now well set up, all he had then was a Rosengart* – and he hadn't finished paying for that! Maurice Tardy had never lacked audacity so came straight out and offered the Ligue a 30,000 francs guarantee (money which he didn't have) plus he signed a five-year exclusive contract with Lyon-Villeurbanne Stadium!

On the morning of 1 May, Maurice Tardy rose at dawn to inspect the sky and read the papers. He tumbled down from his attic room at 5am with the notion of using up all his remaining assets on buying a sprig of lily-of-the-valley. It was raining cats and dogs and the local papers carried the news of a general strike on the trams... absolute disaster! With his sprig of lily-of-the-valley, he climbed back up to his sixth-floor room, resigned to the loss of his Rosengart and even to the damp straw of a prison cell. But from that day on, there was the clearest proof that Maurice Tardy had been born under a lucky star. Miraculously, the rain stopped on the stroke of mid-day, the tram strike was settled and the "gate" came to 57,000 francs.

Not only that, but Max Rousié, good old Maxou, made his début, replacing in succession the pioneers Vignals at scrum-half, then Amila at stand-off. It was a huge success but Maurice Tardy, with a sigh of relief, gave up his five-year exclusive contract with the

*Rosengart: an up-market touring car.

13

stadium to Mr. Pancera, a boxing and speedway promoter and great friend of Delbat, the manager of Stade Buffalo. After the triumphant Yorkshire tour, there was an explosion of rugby league clubs. S. A. Villeneuve followed Jean Galia and Max Rousié, going over to the code en bloc. A splinter group from S. A. Bordelais, led by Messrs. Loze, Queheillard, Pelot and Rosenblat, quit the FFR and founded Bordeaux XIII. With encouragement from pioneers Dechavanne, Duhau and Petit, Gustave Placé, who had inherited a lot of money, and a young industrialist called Claude Devernois who would build a knitwear empire, set up the star-studded Roanne XIII. Always ready for a scrap, the great Marcel Laborde founded XIII Catalan in Perpignan. Rugby league took off and lifted the oval ball game from the depths of mediocrity and sterility of union, starved of international competition. Even Paris caught the rugby league bug. Messrs. Drouet and Clemenceau, whom impudent students had christened 'The Undertakers' for their stern manner and sombre dress, showed plenty of life in founding Paris XIII.

As the game wasn't taken as seriously as it is today, it was welcomed with open arms in the Latin Quarter. The battle of the two rugbys must have been, one suspects, the excuse for many fantastic student pranks. The most restless spirits, unhappy that their Paris University club was far too strict, founded the QEC (Student Quarter Club), with a future minister, Louis Jacquinot, as president. Also among their number was Francis Lopez, later to become a celebrated composer, a young singer who would find fame under the name of André Dassarry and a fine arts student who would become my valued colleague and great friend, Loys Van Lee. Out of respect for historical accuracy we have to point out to his many young female admirers that handsome 'Lolo' was the first player to score a rugby league try in France, in the curtain-raiser to the famous 1933 Australia-England match.

Van Lee was a schoolboy track and field international and a flying winger. Nobody recognized Loys, he of the Viking god blond tresses, when he lined up for the QEC versus SOP game under the name of Eloysa, looking like a scruffy Russian peasant with a beard and wig. Eloysa's contribution was memorable. In the act of scoring the first-ever try in French rugby league for QEC, an SOP player reached out in a desperate effort to grab his jersey but his fingers could only catch hold of the bottom of the wig. Horrified to find Eloysa's hair in his hand, the unfortunate lad fainted on the spot.

So that they could fund a good blow-out at the popular Capoulade café, Van Lee and friends also sold two international athletes who played for QEC, Levier and Dessus, to Paris XIII for the tidy sum of 1,000 francs apiece.

Just like a funicular railway, as rugby league went up, so rugby union declined. The new rugby, bright, fast and sparkling, drew all the union stars one by one, for they were weary of poor-quality internationals against Germany or Romania. The Ligue had just discovered an attacking genius, a young Basque called Jean Dauger, who would go on to forge an historic partnership with the peerless Max Rousié. Another thoroughbred attacker, the Catalan Jep Desclaux, also switched codes and so they could cross the Channel as the true representatives of French rugby. In St Helens, on 25 February 1939, they beat England for the first time, fully deserving their 12-9 victory over the old enemy.

While the Ligue was triumphant, the FFR conference in Marseilles on 24 June 1939, admitted that their numbers had melted like snow in the sun. They only had 471 clubs, whereas in 1930 there had been 784!

Where would rugby union on this side of the Channel be without the Second World War? It may seem paradoxical, but first the war, then the occupation, saved the FFR. More from compulsion than choice, the Second World War led the worthies of the International Board to grant French rugby union a pardon. Of course they did! At the height of the Entente Cordiale, when France and England stood side by side on the same front (despite so many French being so astonished to see so few Tommies dispatched to the banks of the Rhine), they weren't going to glare at one another over an unfortunate incident back in 1931 when the International Board broke off relations.

And so, after some VIPs from the Quai d'Orsay had held a few meetings with their counterparts from the Foreign Office, our British friends sent an expeditionary force, one of the few, said the scandal-mongers. To show how anxious they were to cooperate, the FFR decided to entertain His Gracious Majesty's Forces' team at Parc des Princes. But our lads never left base, they weren't strong enough and the British inflicted a crushing 36-3 defeat. All the same, French officials were happy for this time they could state without a word of a lie (unlike other occasions when they didn't want to hurt the feelings of 'true gentlemen') that the British were still our undisputed masters. What a great return to the fold!

The FFR certainly benefited from catastrophe. War had provided the essential enemy and occupation was going to rid it of an unwanted and dangerous rival. In whose name, under what pretext, through what influence, by what shady deals and by virtue of what principles did the Vichy government decide to ban all games in one sport: rugby league?

I am well aware that the dust of time helps to conceal old injustices, but when will those who love our game feel able to forget this Vichy decree?

Secretary of State for National Education and Youth

No. 5.285 – Decree of 19 December 1941, banning the body called "*Ligue Française de Rugby à XIII.*"
- We, Marshal of France, Head of State,
- In respect of the law of 20 December 1940 regarding sporting organisations,
- On the proposal of the Secretary of State for National Education and Youth,
- Decree:

Article 1 - The aforesaid "*Ligue Française de Rugby à XIII*", Headquarters in Paris at 24, rue Drouot, is banned, its permit having been refused.

Article 2 - The assets of the banned organization, by virtue of the preceding article, are transferred in their entirety to the National Sports Committee. This body will bear total responsibility for them and will appoint its secretary-general, Mr. Charles Denis, Officer of the Legion of Honour, to administer the process of liquidation.

Article 3 - The Secretary of State for National Education and Youth is charged with the execution of the present decree which will be published in the Official Journal.

Ordered at Vichy, 29 December 1941.

Petain.

On behalf of the Marshal of France, Head of State, Secretary of State for National Education and Youth.

Jerome Carcopino.

Who played the rôle of Lady Macbeth? It's a mystery! But one thing is certain: the war between the two rugbys ended with a murder. There are still hands reeking of blood and, as Shakespeare's murderess bemoaned: "All the perfumes of Arabia will not sweeten them".

amazingly opulent and lies in the heart of the city's mini Manhattan, looking out on the main thoroughfares, Philip Street and Elizabeth Street. It rises eight storeys above ground and four under, with an ultra-modern interior boasting two lifts, a hotel, two theatres, 10 bars, lounges, snooker rooms and a bowling alley. 7,500 members have the exclusive right to drink, dance, watch shows, write, read, smoke, amuse themselves generally and finally, pour their shillings into poker machines in the often illusory hope of winning something. Hundreds of Australians wait for a member to die so that they can gain entry to Sydney's *Gotha**. So even obituaries become a source of revenue, for while the deceased obtains his place in heaven, the new member pays hard cash to ensure the future well-being of the NSW Rugby League.

Until 1951, whenever a Kangaroo came over to France, he'd eye our players up and down with an element of condescension, particularly since we'd never managed to beat them in an international. In 1938, the Australians won both tests: 35-6 in Paris to usher in the New Year, and 16-11 in Marseilles a fortnight later, before boarding ship for home at the city's la Joliette docks. Yet that was the era of Rousié, Dauger, Noguères, Chaud, Duran, Brinsolles, Brunetaud, Guiral and, of course, Antoine Blain. It was just the same in 1949: 29-10 in Marseilles for starters and 10-0 in Bordeaux to finish, even though the French team boasted Dop, Crespo, Comes, Calixte, Brousse, Martin, Beraud, Mazon, Contrastin, Caillou, Dejean and Bartoletti among others. All the same, these 'Frenchies' had something which would appeal to the crowds down under – personality - so they were invited over. The French officials had the courage to take it on and agreed to pay all their own expenses, settling for a share of the receipts. In the event, the Australians didn't get a bad deal.

This journey down under was the boldest venture ever attempted by any French national team, whatever the sport. Paul Barrière and Claude Devernois were the ones who had taken all the risks, but had found someone just as daft to share them, my old friend, Antoine Blain, dual-code international and, right up to the end of the war, a sports journalist. He was an explosive mixture of Basque and Catalan, (although, of course, his father-in-law, 'Sultan' Sebedio, might also have passed on some of his own extraordinary temperament as part of the dowry), but one thing was certain: my friend Antoine was a superman, an unusual combination of brute force, a sense of humour that was alternately French and British, lively intelligence, bubbling dynamism and the ability to sustain an unbelievable workload.

Gotha: France's equivalent of *Who's Who*, i.e. all the important people.

At the same, time he was a bit of a lad, capable of downing 12 pints or two dozen whiskies at will and entertaining an audience with some nifty conjuring tricks. Can you see why Antoine Blain was the man to lead this expedition? When Adolphe Jaureguy met him before he left, he said: "When I think of you venturing into the unknown, I have to wonder if you're mad." "Hold on, you're talking like my wife," replied Antoine with a smile.

The French party took off from Marseilles' Marignane airport at midday on Monday 14 May. It was 30 strong: Antoine Blain (manager), Jean Duhau and Robert Samatan (coaches) and 27 players:

Full-backs: Puig-Aubert (Carcassonne) and André (Marseilles).
Wingers: Contrastin and Lespes (Bordeaux), Cantoni (Toulouse).
Centres: Merquey (Marseilles), Comes (XIII Catalan), Caillou (Toulouse), Crespo (Lyons).
Stand-offs: Bellan (Lyons), Galaup (Albi).
Scrum-halves: Dop (Marseilles), Duffort (Lyons).
Props: Mazon (Carcassonne), Beraud and Rinaldi (Marseilles), Bartoletti (Bordeaux).
Hookers: Martin (Carcassonne), Genoud (Villeneuve), Audoubert (Lyons).
Second-rows: Brousse and Montrucolis (Lyons), Ponsinet (Carcassonne), Delaye (Marseilles).
Loose-forwards: Perez (Marseilles), Calixte (Villeneuve), Lopez (Cavaillon).

Actually, only 29 were on the flight because young Galaup was still in the forces, had not yet got permission to travel and was forced to join his colleagues in Sydney a week later. Their departure was unbelievably low-key, without the scrum of cameramen one normally meets on big sporting occasions. One photograph, just one single photograph, more suitable for the family album than posterity, and that was it! Only a few weeks later, the Australians were swearing that this was the finest team in the history of rugby league.

Pen pictures of the 1951 tourists

1. Puig-Aubert (Carcassonne) Vice-captain. Full-back. 11 stone; 5 feet 3 inches; 25; Representative. A genius. Nicknamed Pipette in his youth after his thin, rolled cigarettes, he also loves pastis and hates training. Superb goalkicker who can also drop goals from his own half. This tricky runner is a real world star.
2. Ode Lespes (Bordeaux) Wing. 12 stone 10 pounds; 5 feet 11 inches; 27; Representative. A real speed merchant whose dazzlingside-steps have bamboozled many an opponent. Prolific try scorer despite suffering six fractured collarbones in a season and a half.
3. Gaston Comes (XIII Catalan) Centre or full-back. 11 stone 11 pounds; 5 feet 8 inches; 28; Café proprietor. Uncompromising on defence, he is

also a brilliant attacker with a marvellous dummy. Elusive and quick, he can slip through the tightest of defences.

4. Jackie Merquey (Marseilles) Centre. 11 stone; 5 feet 5 inches; 22; Pharmaceutical student. Great centre who seems to defend superbly without doing too much tackling. Tricky runner who creates gaps and puts colleagues away. Class individual who is also a team man. Had to miss June examinations to tour.

5. Vincent Cantoni (Toulouse) Wing. 12 stone 4 pounds; 5 feet 9 inches; 24; Tradesman. Aggressive runner and cruel tackler, 'Nano' won his first cap in 1948 against the touring Australians. Has proved himself a determined finisher with a great sidestep and clever kick-ahead.

6. Charles Galaup (Albi) Half-back or centre. 12 stone 4 pounds; 5 feet 8 inches; 22; Civil servant. Currently on leave from national service, he arrived later than the others after forgetting to ask for permission to tour. Lively and skilful player, whose pace and deceptive running are real assets to any team.

7. Jean Dop (Marseilles) Scrum-half. 11 stone 11 pounds; 5 feet 5 inches; 30; Barman. Unpredictable will o' the wisp. This talented Basque match-winner, nicknamed 'Devil's Brother', is a law unto himself – and with his own sense of humour. Perhaps best described as "very emotional".

8. Louis Mazon (Carcassonne) Prop. 13 stone 8 pounds; 5 feet 9 inches; 30; Council employee. Experts regard 'Lolo' as the finest post-war French prop. Not the biggest, but skilful, brave and durable. Respected by hard men everywhere. Resistance fighter who was captured, beaten up but escaped.

9. Martin Martin (Carcassonne) Front-row. 13 stone 2 pounds; 5 feet 7 inches; 28; Truck driver. Solid Basque from Boucau, nicknamed 'The Spaniard'. Very effective in the loose, with aggressive tackling, tricky runs and the best dummy in France. His aggression has been known to get him into trouble.

10. André Beraud (Marseilles) Prop. 13 stone 11 pounds; 5 feet 10 inches; 29; Foreman in a sugar refinery. Basque centre who converted successfully to the prop position. Pack leader at Marseilles, and a superb craftsman whose ball-handling skills and pace from his centre days make him something special.

11. Elie Brousse (Lyons) Second-row. 15 stone 4 pounds; 6 feet 1 inch; 29; Foreman in the silk spinning industry. Possibly the best second-row in the world, this Catalan giant is exceptional on attack, hunting behind his backs. Defensively magnificent, sweeping tirelessly in his cover role. Amazing speed and agility for one so big.

12. Edouard Ponsinet (Carcassonne) Second-row. 14 stone 9 pounds; 5 feet 10 inches; 27; Draughtsman. 'Ponpon' is a rarity – a super-athlete (11.4 seconds for 100 metres) transformed into a world-class rugby player. At full gallop, he's practically impossible to stop. Awesome. Also an enthusiastic boxer.

13. Gaston Calixte (Villeneuve) Loose-forward. 13 stone 10 pounds; 6 feet; 27; Café proprietor. His outstanding technique is admired throughout the game. Reads a game superbly and talks others through it. He began his international career on the wing, so speed is another of his assets.

25

14. René Duffort (Lyons) Loose-forward or half-back. 13 stone 8 pounds; 5 feet 9 inches; 27; Painter. Solid and skilful all-rounder who instigates many of the moves. Fine reader of a game and holds all the parts together. A place for him in any team.

15. Raymond Contrastin (Bordeaux) Wing. 11 stone 11 pounds; 5 feet 8 inches; 26; PE instructor. Muscular pocket-battleship. Especially quick over 30 yards. Brave and direct: he takes the shortest route to the line. Known as 'Tintin', he won't show his face if the team loses.

16. Maurice André (Marseilles) Full-back or threequarter. 11 stone 7 pounds; 5 feet 8 inches; 29; Clerk in police service. Tremendous tackler who is also a dangerous counter-attacker. Equally at home at centre or on the wing, he is also a fine goal-kicker.

17. Robert Caillou (Toulouse) Tour captain. Centre or half-back. 11 stone 11 pounds; 5 feet 9 inches; 33; Café proprietor. A deadly tackler who can also open up the tightest defences. Grew up next to the town hall in his native Bayonne where a stadium was named after him.

18. Maurice Bellan (Lyons) Half-back. 11 stone 12 pounds; 5 feet 11 inches; Thoroughbred attacker who can hold down any position in the backs thanks to his lightning pace, nose for an opening and fine kicking game.

19. Raoul Perez (Marseilles) Loose-forward. 14 stone 9 pounds; 6 feet; 27; Representative. An opportunist with exceptional all-round talent. 'The Gipsy' may seem nonchalant, but his stunning sidestep and amazing acceleration spell danger for any unwary defence.

20. Michael Lopez (Cavaillon) Back-row. 16 stone; 6 feet 1 inch; 31; Market gardener. This fine athlete has had the bad luck to be in the shadow of the great Brousse-Ponsinet partnership, but he is technically very sound in his own right.

21. Guy Delaye (Marseilles) Second-row. 14 stone 9 pounds; 6 feet 1 inch; 21; Porter. A real powerhouse who comes up with some devastating charges. Very skilful and effective, even if he looks plump.

22. François Montrucolis (Lyons) Second-row. 15 stone 1 pound; 5 feet 10 inches; 26; Electrician. Always in the thick of battle. Rugged, durable and no respecter of reputations. When he charges, you can count the bodies. Very mobile for a big man.

23. Paul Bartoletti (Bordeaux) Hooker or prop. 13 stone 5 pounds; 5 feet 9 inches; 24; Tradesman. Small for a prop, but brave and highly mobile. Defensively uncompromising and dubbed 'The Lion of Wembley' for his outstanding performance there in 1949.

24. Jean Audoubert (Lyons) Hooker or prop. 14 stone 10 pounds; 5 feet 10 inches; 27; Hosiery worker. Known as 'Monseigneur' because of the roundness of his silhouette, he preaches the gospel of giving back double whatever comes his way. Tough, uncompromising forward who is remarkably adept at the turning pass.

25. Gabriel Genoud (Villeneuve) Hooker. 12 stone 10 pounds; 5 feet 7 inches; 28; Grocer. Technically excellent. A bustler in the loose, 'Gaby's' intelligent contributions add so much to the team's performance. Accomplished ball-winner.

26. François Rinaldi (Marseilles) Prop. 13 stone 9 pounds; 5 feet 11 inches; 26; Tradesman. Fine amateur boxer before turning to rugby. On the field, he's tough and direct - a real athlete - but so handsome, the press have compared him to Burt Lancaster.

27. Jo Crespo (Lyons) Half-back or threequarter. 11 stone 10 pounds; 5 feet 7 inches; 26; Business representative. This Catalan is a complete player: merciless on defence and full of invention on attack. The team's pivot and a splendid distributor who combines especially well with club-mate René Duffort.

Antoine Blain (Manager) Dual-code international. Second-row in the first French team to play Australia and in that which beat England for the first time in 1939. After distinguished war service, he coached Carcassonne for five successful years before concentrating on journalism. 'The Turk' is liked and respected everywhere rugby is played.

Jean Duhau (Coach) Brilliant forward who won international caps in both codes. One of Galia's 'Pioneers' in 1934 when he was promised a trip to Australia. It took 17 years to come true! Spent five years in a prisoner-of-war camp, losing seven stones in the process. Has enjoyed a successful coaching career and is renowned for his man-management.

Bob Samatan (Coach) Distinguished dual-code international and, like his great friend Duhau, a 'Pioneer'. Smart player and excellent tactician who has enjoyed great success as a coach, including taking his current champions, Lyons, to the recent cup final.

Puig-Aubert and Guy Delaye watching a 1951 match.

Vincent Cantoni tackles an opponent on the 1951 tour.
(Both courtesy Louis Bonnery)

Someone called Puig-Aubert

The natives found the sight of French rugby players in Australia as curious as the arrival of Montesquieu's* Persians in Versailles.

Before being paraded before a huge crowd at the Sydney Cricket Ground, the Tricolors were allowed a little three-match excursion around New South Wales, all of which they won. In the first at Canberra, against Monaro Division, the margin was a comfortable 37-12. Newcastle offered stiffer opposition before going down 12-8 while, in the third, the tough Western Province selection were only just pipped 26-24 at Forbes.

Finally, the day came when the Sydneysiders had their first glimpse of France at the holy of holies, Sydney Cricket Ground. Its curious stands adorned with rococo clocktowers were evidence enough of how long rugby league on the Pacific coasts had prospered.

The Tricolors' headquarters was the modest Olympic Hotel overlooking an avenue of palm trees leading to the stadium on the other side of Moore Park Road. They were astonished to see crowds gathering since the gates opened at nine in the morning. Only the 20,000 seat members' stand was empty, in which the fortunate owners of a metal badge were guaranteed a seat for life for £200. They could linger in a private bar, reeking of tobacco and beer like a wild west saloon and so big you could fit Saint-Lazare station concourse in it. With so much smooth Australian draught lager gushing over the huge counter, the barmen, too, were under pressure, but the hubbub died away as the French team, led by Antoine Blain, Jean Duhau and Bob Samatan, passed in front of the big entrance door to go through to the dressing rooms opposite.

It was an unusual dressing room, huge and comfortable with glazed sliding doors opening on to a balcony big enough for all the team to sit and watch the preliminary games. You could relax there as if on a veranda and welcome press and officials. The walls were lined with old framed photos including one of Dally Messenger, 'The Master', and another of the Cricket Ground absolutely jam-packed during an Australia versus England cricket test. At the rear were two enormous rooms where the players changed and had rub-downs, while showers and baths stood on a mezzanine platform.

"Shit! This beats Carcassonne!" quipped Puig-Aubert. But the team didn't feel in the mood for jokes. The surroundings, enthusiasm of the crowd and reception which had greeted their

---

*Montesquieu: wrote in 1721 about two Persian brothers who came to France and became the subject of much curiosity.

appearance on the balcony had been so foreign that some even felt like it was a double-or-quits game: beat Sydney, who were just as strong as the full Australian team, and they could beat anyone. They had left France without much ceremony, a bit like the penniless Basques who had set off for the Americas in the hope of making their fortune. Could they, then, manage such a feat?

The Australians were totally confident that star-studded Sydney would win without having to extend themselves too much. They were looking forward with a mixture of amusement and curiosity to seeing these funny Frenchmen who, it was said, played a strange game very different from the pragmatic Kangaroos. The Sydney crowd, however, would not quickly forget the first time they saw the 'Unpredictable French'.

At least France had learned something about Australians from the first three matches – the opening minutes would be played at a frantic pace. For five minutes the Australians launched themselves like demons, battering the French defence like crazed rams. The trial of strength was even harder to win because these Kangaroo devils never lost possession, so there was only one thing to do: let the storm blow itself out and protect the try line at all costs. Arms, legs, backs all ached with the non-stop impact, but they clenched their teeth and nothing got past. You see, we had men like Crespo and Cantoni to put their bodies on the line and topple any Australian who thought he was through.

Eventually the early fire was doused and Sydney had only managed to notch a solitary Bernie Purcell penalty goal. The crowd were beside themselves, for they loved it when man rediscovered his primitive ferocity and were mad keen on the crowning glory of rugby league – the physical battle. Sydney hadn't won yet, but surely they had laid the foundations for triumph with a whirlwind start which had left the French weakened, breathless and with the bitter taste of defeat already in their mouths. The sporting crowd had already been applauding what they believed was a pointless display of courage, as they believed the tourists were beaten, when they were astonished to see a supposedly vanquished French team launch a cheeky counterattack. Throwing the ball about with bewildering speed, their furious attacks created panic in the opposition. The Tricolors were unstoppable. The ball fizzed everywhere, but there was always a blue jersey backing up.

Twice in as many minutes, Genoud and Crespo raced over for tries and the stunned crowd watched in astonishment as the incredible Puig-Aubert teed the ball up without even looking at the posts, turned towards his own line and, after a short run-up, lazily booted it skyward between the uprights. What cheek! What an affront to rugby etiquette as formulated by the all-conquering

British Empire! A gentleman wouldn't have done that! Australians, for whom sport was meat and drink, couldn't believe what Antoine Blain's men were doing before their very eyes, here in their own backyard. They clapped because they appreciated what was happening, but it was so exceptional that they just waited for the inevitable collapse.

'Unpredictable France's' 10-2 lead was something they simply hadn't expected. Confident in their physical prowess, the Australians dug deep and began the long haul back. They threatened, but could only score another penalty, cutting the gap to 10-4. Once again, the Australian storm blew over and gave way to a French surge. Cantoni, on the end of a passing movement, looked like being thrown over the left touchline when an unbelievable burst took him past three defenders to dive over in the corner. Now the crowd began to believe in the French miracle and exploded when Pipette put the conversion over. 15-4 was more than a possible win, it was a revelation! Incredible as the try had been, it didn't do the French cause much good for overconfidence set in. Thinking victory was in the bag, the Tricolor defence fell away and they learned a hard lesson: Australians are a breed apart.

"You've got to shoot them three times to be sure they're dead," declared Jean Duhau, and he was right. France thought they could take a breather but, before they knew it, Sydney had scored twice and closed to 15-14. That was all it needed to lift the whole stadium to fever pitch and the Australians were on a roll. Then France used her secret weapon, Pipette's boot, and he landed a monumental drop-goal from just inside the Sydney half.

Leading 17-14, France believed they were on track for a win which had looked beyond them, but the Australians had other ideas, and launched attack after blistering attack until minutes seemed like centuries.

"How long to go? How long?" shouted Pipette to Jean Duhau and Bob Samatan who were gnawing their nails on the touchline: "Seven, six, five," the coaches called out, fingers held up to make the message clearer. With four minutes left, a frantic roar went up as the huge centre Gordon Willoughby heaved himself out of a desperate Tricolor tackle and hurtled towards the French line. Ponsinet and Puig-Aubert came across to cut him off but Willoughby used all of his 15 stone to crash over in the corner. Sydney were level at 17-17 and the crowd went wild.

Bernie Purcell took meticulous care over the conversion attempt from touch as do all the Anglo-Saxon kickers, but Australians in particular. In the stands, the betting was steady on 5 to 1 against him landing it from such an acute angle. Propped on its little pile of soil, the ball looked like a shell pointing at the French posts.

Everyone held his breath. The ball defied the angle to soar between the uprights. 19-17! Purcell's conversion had turned Willoughby's equaliser into out-and-out victory. The crowd was overcome with the emotion of it all and got ready to make for the exits. France put up a furious last-ditch effort. Once, twice they could have come up with the try that would have changed everything, but missed by a whisker. Over there, on the opposite side from the Members' Stand, the Hill, that massive mound of earth covered with a tide of humanity, began to show the first signs of thinking it was all over.

The die was cast. Already savouring their boys' triumph, the good folk of Sydney hadn't noticed that, at the moment the bell rang, the referee had awarded France a penalty right on halfway. They all thought it a bit of a joke to see a little full-back called Puig-Aubert come up for the kick, the sort of amusement one feels towards someone cheeky enough to take on a lost cause. Only Duhau and Samatan bothered to bite their nails. Pipette picked the ball up with a hand amazingly large for one so small and with the other gestured towards the posts. Touch judges ran to their stations. Pipette launched a drop-kick with a casualness every Australian expert labelled criminal, but they changed their minds the moment the ball rose, as if propelled by some supernatural force. To a deafening roar, France had snatched a draw, but Australia had discovered Pipette and went on to make him a demi-God.

The day after this spectacular game, the Australian press heaped plaudits on the Tricolors. In the *Daily Telegraph*, Frank O'Rourke wrote: "The big question about the French tourists' quality, or lack of it, has been well and truly answered. Sydney has never seen such spontaneous skills as the French displayed in the first half. The pack, solid and speedy, played a perfect game and prompted attacks by their white-hot backs. The visitors popped up all over the pitch with pace and skill the like of which we've certainly never seen here before."

The French had arrived. They had been given the once-over and had passed muster. From now on they would be the 'Flying Frenchmen' but, head and shoulders above the rest, Puig-Aubert reached a pinnacle of fame that would not fade with the passing of time.

In the *Sydney Morning Herald* Tom Goodman hailed him the hero of the hour: "The fantastic goal that the little full-back, Puig-Aubert, landed after the bell sounded was the highlight of an incredibly exciting match."

At the height of his fame, Pipette's kicking made national headlines. Every Australian paper carried a cartoon showing Puig-Aubert screwing a drop-goal over his own posts off his own try-line while the Australian pack, red in the face, raised their arms to the heavens and claimed, "He certainly deserves a KB!" A KB, by the way, is a well-known beer: Tooth's KB Lager. To become the star of a beer advert within a single day is as remarkable in Australia as making it into Madame Tussaud's here while you're still living. This is, however, the right moment to establish that KB was in no way to blame for the phenomenal stoutness which, in the years to come, turned Pipette globe-shaped, for pastis was still his preferred tipple by a mile. If KB Lager had appealed to him, he would perhaps have accepted the fabulous offers which the Australian clubs were to make but, as we've said, he preferred pastis, a drink which had not yet won over the Antipodeans.

After storming Sydney, France's next game was eagerly anticipated. Just think: people who play rugby like artists, who turn their backs on the posts before a kick, who eat frog's legs and snails, that's a sure-fire winner! Curiosity reached a peak when the Press laid siege to the Olympic Hotel headquarters and revealed that the French were not following any régime. They were drinking three or four glasses of red wine with every meal, eating enormous bloody steaks and to improve the menu, the great prop, Lolo Mazon, was cooking wild duck which Martin, Dop, Comes and Contrastin had killed with catapults in the local parks.

Contrastin even scared my colleague Jim Mathers of the *Daily Mirror* when, after swallowing a good half-pint of Australian Burgundy, he smacked his lips with pleasure and growled, "That's what does your stomach good!"

Jim Mathers was very worried and went to see Jean Duhau to tell him that Contrastin was surely going to be ill. "He's drunk a half of red, did you say? That's nothing. At home in Condom he distills Armagnac, but never bothers about selling any – he drinks it all himself!" Mathers stood open-mouthed, convinced that Contrastin was going to go down with *delirium tremens* on the pitch during the next Test. That night of 9 June 1951 was warm. In Sydney, the approach of winter is called 'Indian Summer' and it really is mild. The sun is less strong and the ground, which had been crying out for rain for the last five months, exuded a pleasant warmth.

Antoine Blain couldn't sleep; he never could before a big game. He went out of room number 1, the one Jack Mason reserved for VIPs because it had the benefit of its own bathroom, and noticed that there was still a light on in Jean Duhau's room across the corridor. No doubt Duhau was sorting out jerseys for he always made sure the night before a game that each player would wear the right number and the right size of shorts, not the voluminous sort in which English teams of yore sailed.

He peeped round the door and there was Duhau, counting and recounting his clobber.

"Now, Jean, not in bed yet?"

"No. You see, Antoine, I'm going through the equipment. You know them, those buggers, tomorrow they'll ransack everything. 'My shorts are too long. There's holes in my socks. My number's coming off.' You know what I said to the moaners last Saturday?"

"No, tell me."

"Well, I asked them that in future, when we're invited to a dance, they try and find a girlfriend who can sew a bit, for I've never yet come across a woman who wants to mend our kit. We're going to end up bare-arsed with these wild Australians who rip everything to shreds. For the first test tomorrow, you see, I want our turn-out to be immaculate for when you feel good, you play better."

"Yes, and we'll need all the help we can get. These Kangaroos frighten me, Jean. Physically, they've definitely got the edge. It's going to be a massive trial of strength. If we play them at their own game, we've no chance. We'll not hold them in the second half. We have to retain possession and that's why the better hooker, Genoud, has been picked in preference to Martin who is superior in the loose. While we have the ball we must avoid being tackled, quicken the game up to get them out of breath and take these giants on with sheer speed. At the same time, when we're pinned down under our own sticks, we need Puig-Aubert free to put in one of those raking kicks of his. Without these breathers, our pack won't last the game. But we'll go over all this in more detail tomorrow with Samatan and the team. I'll let you get some sleep."

"Hypocrite! You know damn well I never sleep. If sometimes I close my eyes, it's only because of dust. The night before a game, I'm all worked up. I've been like that since I was 16 and made my senior debut at Boucau Stade. What you want is for me to buy you a drink down in the bar before it shuts at 10 o'clock."

Antoine's smile was confirmation and down they went to the bar. It was certainly an interesting pub that Jack Mason ran on the ground floor of the Olympic Hotel. A strong smell of beer hung permanently over the vast room where, from opening to closing time, dedicated drinkers congregated two and three deep round a big horseshoe bar. There were quiet ones who drank alone, not speaking a word but downing seven pints an hour. Others loved company, and offered to buy their neighbours a round, knowing full well that they'd get one back before their glass was empty. What both needed - the fundamental, as the philosopher would say - was a quick dash to the gents. This was what the third category, the seated drinkers, lacked.

I have long suspected the drinkers seated to the right of the bar of having a problem with their bladders. They are lost in silent thought before a glass that is never full and rarely empty, waiting quietly until they are put out at closing time. Not good customers, these, managing a pint only every 15 minutes. Real party-poopers!

As the Olympic is also a place to go to for entertainment, they have an ancient piano that sounds as though it should be in a dance hall, on which a pre-war beauty executes, literally and figuratively, pieces chosen for their faded appeal. That's why we no longer count the times when, to please the Tricolors, she's massacred "J'attendrai", "C'est si bon" and "Sous les ponts de Paris". On Friday, pay-day, consumption reaches such levels that Jack Mason has to put on the glazed entrance door a notice, with a black border as if announcing a bereavement, stating: "No Beer". It comes as a nasty shock to any thirsty fellow who makes the oasis, so both door and landlord's eardrums take a bit of a hammering. Well, the next pub is miles away!

Blain and Duhau were instantly recognisable, one in his blue France blazer, the other, as always, in his tracksuit with the cockerel badge. Of course, they were the instant centre of attraction in the bar. Offered drinks and more drinks, treated to much backslapping by would-be friends and torn between those who wanted autographs, badges or simply a prediction, our manager and coach needed every ounce of strength from their former front-row frames to survive.

Antoine Blain even allowed himself the luxury of a counterattack. He offered a round of drinks and performed a few conjuring tricks which brought belly-laughs galore. Duhau, on the other hand, had great difficulty extricating himself from his admirers and had to employ his whole armoury of English: "Tomorrow... After the game... Yes, yes, Australia very good... France good team, yes, yes. Win perhaps." Nothing could break up his circle of admirers. "In God's name, I don't know how I managed to extricate myself, for instead of beating them off, I seemed to attract more! I thought the buggers were going to strip me!"

Jean Duhau was saved by the bell for 10 o'clock closing time. A hefty six-footer, well over 16 stones, whose job was obviously to empty the place of customers, clapped his great paws and bellowed in a voice which echoed round the room, "Gentlemen! Gentlemen!"

The mark of an Australian drinker is to face adversity with dignity and respect the rules. One by one, the circles broke up and customers disappeared into the night, tucking under their arms bottles of beer, discreetly wrapped in newspaper, which they had had the foresight to buy before closing time from the bottles department. Blain and Duhau were the last to leave but, at the door, a funny little old man who had clearly had one too many, poked his finger in Antoine Blain's chest: "Kangaroos strong, very strong. The best, always the best in the world. Frenchies…" The old fellow turned his thumb towards the ground in a gesture which needed no translation.

"There's one who'll not be putting his shirt on us," remarked Duhau philosophically.

Sydney is the Casablanca of the Southern Seas and the huge palm trees in Moore Park Road barely rustled in the gentle sea breeze. Blain and Duhau went out on to the pavement and lit cigarettes. From the corner, you could see the lights of the city, but their eyes were instinctively drawn towards the Cricket Ground there, below them, on the other side of the street.

"What the hell's that?" Duhau burst out. Had a gigantic swarm of fireflies settled on the stadium terraces? The mass of glowing insects was fantastical, like something from a dream. In reality, it was quite simply the thousands of fans who, to secure a good 'spec', had already taken their places on the terraces and were smoking to kill time. Never, in more that 25 years of international rugby, had Blain and Duhau seen anything so extraordinary, and they found themselves crossing the road for a closer look.

What an incredible vigil! Just 100 yards away, the French team lay asleep and here, a colossal encampment had formed. The enemy had already claimed their ground and they were more than ready for the Tricolors. Absolutely amazing – 15,000 Australians bivouacked around the pitch with their snacks, beer and whisky. You really have to be in Sydney for a test match to appreciate the Australian passion for rugby.

Despite last Saturday's brilliant display, the French officials were somewhat unnerved by this spectacle. Blain and Duhau hardly exchanged a word on the way back to the hotel, but the same question puzzled them. Could 13 French rugby players, all on their own, take on a whole nation?

French champagne rugby

"Papers! Papers!" The little paper boy climbed the Olympic Hotel's two floors and announced a new day. Saturday, 10 June 1951, was no ordinary day, but the big day, a day with a capital D. That's why his cry was met by a bigger torrent of abuse and curses than usual. "Papers! Papers!" he continued, used to responses like that and, as usual, he only had the one customer, Antoine Blain, who took the two dailies, the *Sydney Morning Herald* and the *Daily Telegraph*. Both had brought out an Australia versus France special edition, but his morning tea tasted bitter as Antoine noted that both offered the same opinion: "Australian power will destroy the French artists' dream by the second half."

Poor 'Flying Frenchmen!', soon to be another trophy in the invincible Kangaroos' extensive collection. Numbers never lie, as Anglo-Saxons always say, but what about last Saturday's fabulous 19-19 draw against Sydney? They had forgetten the overconfidence and carelessness after France led 10-2 at half-time. Experts thought it just a draw snatched in the last second by an exceptional Puig-Aubert goal. Sure, they found time to praise the display and applaud the panache, but how could a national team which couldn't beat Sydney overcome the full might of Australia?

How can you believe that when, let's be honest, they hadn't come to terms with a tough schedule of successive high-tempo games? Why, it was only last Tuesday they'd lost for the first time, 20-10, against Riverina Division in Albury.

Without doubt, the conquerors of Sydney had disappointed in Albury, but you have to remember that the Tricolors, unlike the English, New Zealanders and Australians, don't always put out their best team. That being the case, and suspecting France might suffer a setback, Antoine Blain, Jean Duhau and Bob Samatan had decided to field in Albury as few as possible of those selected for the first test. That was why only two chosen for the match four days later played against Riverina: Puig-Aubert and Merquey. Antoine leaned with his elbows on the window sill, watching dawn break on a great festival of rugby. The rising sun lit terraces already packed and full of colour. Only that huge mound, the Hill, was still green and empty. There, standing in the cheapest section, you'd really taste the emotion, far from the comfortable seats where posh people were parked. But to avoid too many cases of sunstroke, the Hill would not be opened till 9 o'clock, just before the first of seven curtain-raisers kicked off. Even for tough Aussies, eight hours on your feet watching rugby was enough.

Queues formed at the turnstiles for the last places and it was a bonanza for the hot-dog sellers. The Hill's gates opened and, within minutes, a tide of humanity swamped the green knoll. Everything was ready for the big event. The stadium was packed to the limit the police had fixed to avoid terraces overflowing like they had in the Australia versus Great Britain match in 1928, when 70,000 paying spectators plus 22,000 life members crammed in. The huge oval, while it was a little worn in the middle from being used for cricket in the summer, was in excellent condition. A funny-looking town band in black trousers, red jackets and spotless colonial helmets welcomed the Kangaroos with *Colonel Bogey*, which had not yet become clichéd from its use in the famous film, *Bridge on the River Kwai*. Finally, the Tricolors straggled out on to the turf to the bouncy *Can-Can* tune which, in the eyes of the Anglo-Saxon world in general, and the Australians in particular, personified French vivacity, gaiety, bubbly personality, charm, oh, and throw in carefree nature for good measure.

There was a nice look about this French team. In the front row, they went for the infectious will-to-win of Mazon, Genoud's technique at hooker and the explosiveness of Bartoletti over the power and skill of Beraud, Martin and Rinaldi. A Brousse and Ponsinet second-row was seen as the trump card, the key to the game. At loose-forward, René Duffort was regarded as successor to Perez, 'The Gipsy', and Calixte, 'The Organiser', being a strategist, leader of men and a fine distributor who would keep to the gameplan.

Though Crespo had done nothing wrong, the selectors preferred the brilliant Dop at scrum-half, hoping that his darting runs and cheeky promptings might bemuse the huge Australians. Galaup was a confident choice at stand-off, the baby of the party and a tremendous prospect. He'd arrived after most of the others, having only realized at the last moment that a soldier had to be granted leave of absence, even if it was for active service in Australia. Explosive Gaston Gomes and dazzling Jackie Merquey were the centres with two big-hitters, Cantoni and Contrastin, the form choices on the wings.

Finally, at full-back, the king – Pipette. We looked solid up front and had backs who could offer pace and the unorthodox. And yet, with the exception of Brousse and Ponsinet, when the teams lined up, ours looked like schoolboys alongside the enormous Australians.

This impressive Australian side seemed unbeatable, with the famous Clive Churchill at full-back and a threequarter line of brick outhouses, the smallest of whom must have weighed around 14 stones. On the wings they had Bliss, national 100 metres sprint champion and Graves, while the centres were Willoughby and Hazzard. Stanmore at stand-off and Holman at scrum-half formed the best partnership in Australia. Finally, up front, we faced six colossal removal men: Crocker at loose-forward, Mulligan and Brian Davies in the second-row, Duncan Hall and Donoghue propping, while the hooker, who went by the evocative name of Schubert, certainly knew how to 'play the mandolin' – a euphemism used in rugby for those who were over-fond of taking heads off.

To sum up, if Hollywood had been looking for a job-lot of hard cases, these six forwards wouldn't have disappointed them. This was the team that lined up, on 10 June 1951, to defend Australia's reputation for invincibility.

Blain, Duhau and Samatan went over the gameplan one more time in the changing-room. "Play it tight while they've got the ball, but when it's your turn, give it some air, throw it about, take 'em on with your speed. Above all, don't just bash into them, forget brute force, it'll be like running into a brick wall and you'll fold in the second half."

The referee, Mr MacMahon, was strict and didn't like anyone trying it on so the Tricolors were on their guard. As expected, the Kangaroos went on the attack with bulldozer tactics, but the French defended efficiently, tackling hard and low. The crowd was absolutely lapping it up, and roars of excitement rang round the ground as it became clear that this would be no walkover. The Australians were being tested to the full and had to come up with a big game for these Frenchies were in no way overawed. Then, within a few minutes, five to be exact, a drama unfolded.

Three Kangaroo play-the-balls, three penalties, three Puig-Aubert goals and France led 6-0. It was a real blow to Australian pride yet the wonderful home crowd gave Pipette a huge ovation. They'd already realised he was something special and savoured everything he did even if it might lead to their favourites' defeat. Six points in the bag and France were following the gameplan to the letter. Safety first, adventure later. The French cockerel was spreading its wings but must have seemed more like an imperial eagle to the SCG crowd. It was going like a dream. The ball pinged from wing to wing and the massive Australians didn't know which way to turn. It was David and Goliath all over again. Skilful and lively, the cheeky Dop, Galaup, Comes and Merquey were in complete control. The pitch seemed full of little imps in red, white and blue sneaking their way past a powerful green wall. One attack had hardly subsided when another was launched on the wing opposite. Something had to give. Groggy, worn out by the frantic tempo, the Australians cracked. With passes fluttering from man to man, Cantoni found himself unmarked 50 yards out and sprinted on down the empty touchline. Full-back Churchill suddenly popped up on the 25. His path to the line narrowed before his very eyes. Was he going to be knocked in touch? No! The winger broke the tackle and dived over in triumph by the corner flag. The infallible Puig-Aubert landed a tricky touchline conversion and France led 11-0.

Now the Tricolors were really piling it on and two minutes after Cantoni's try, prop Lolo Mazon broke and fed the chunky winger, Contrastin. Shaven-headed and with nothing fancy about him, he was a Duhau disciple, believing that the aim of rugby is to get over your opponents' line by the shortest route. He tore through, and when his opposite number, Bliss, hurled himself into the tackle, 'Tintin's' famous hand-off knocked him sprawling four yards away. Ball still tucked under his arm, he raced on. Could anything stop him now?

Yet again, Churchill tried to succeed with our man from Bordeaux where he had failed with Cantoni. With Holman coming to help him, they were dashing to head off Contrastin when the stadium suddenly exploded. Australians love out-and-out brute force and determination and Tintin was going to provide the perfect example. Churchill and Holman threw themselves into the tackle two or three yards from the line, but Contrastin smashed straight through them. While he was scoring in the corner, Churchill was eating dust and poor Holman was flat on his back. The crowd was stunned, amazed by Contrastin's try which so epitomised French team spirit. Marvelling at how the visitors were playing, they forgot that this try and Puig-Aubert's subsequent conversion had just about finished off Australian hopes - 16-0!

Australia had never been so humiliated and yet the crowd were applauding the Tricolors. That day, the Sydney Cricket Ground showed the world sportsmanship at its best. Still shaken by the phenomenal French display, the crowd hardly seemed to notice that a penalty by the winger Graves, just before half-time, had reduced the deficit to 16-2. France left the field to thunderous applause. On the terraces, people stood on their benches and shouted, "Well done, France!" In the dressingroom, the rest of the squad embraced the heroes of the hour. Perez hugged his mate Dop, Crespo threw his arms round Puig-Aubert and physio Bill Moore was all fingers and thumbs strapping up Mazon. In short, it was utter euphoria.

But you've got to watch out for Australians: they're like their boomerangs and nearly always come back at you. They can melt away and then, suddenly, there they'd be, as large as life. Blain, Duhau and Samatan dreaded this euphoria like the plague.

"I'm rather sorry our boys have been so much on top. They can quite easily lose it all just because they think the game's already

The tour becomes a crusade

Although they had won a battle, the Tricolors had a long way to go before their first campaign in Australia could be counted a total success. Now regarded more as invincible super-champions than popular tourists, all future opponents would be desperate to beat them. From now on, it would be a life-or-death struggle to overcome regional teams who would play out of their skins to win a place in history. Any remaining illusions rapidly disappeared on Tuesday 13 June, three days after the memorable first test.

Strangely enough, on-field temperatures rose in Armidale, high up behind the Blue Mountains north of Sydney and one of the coldest spots in Australia. Despite every decision going the way of the home team (in Australia, just like everywhere else), France beat Northern Division comfortably 29-12. Delaye, Crespo, Rinaldi, Lespes, Lopez and Brousse, with two, registered seven tries while, despite generous refereeing, Northern Division could only manage two tries by Madden and Murphy, and three goals by stand-off Fraser. As the final whistle approached, the locals began to take exception to the humiliation and "opened the thump-box".

The Tricolors were no angels in the wholesale fracas that ensued and joined in with a will. In short, both teams were to blame but the referee only saw French punches and, a few minutes from the end, dismissed Audoubert for displaying "an incorrect attitude to an opponent". Although he came from Saint-Girons, it was because of the episcopal scale of his stomach that he was nick-named 'Monseigneur' and not from any angelic disposition. If you gave him a clout on the jaw, he'd give you two back. So Monseigneur was shown the door by a referee with very few Catholic leanings.

Very soon after, the tour captain, Caillou, suffered a deep scalp wound from an Australian boot. Delaye rushed to his aid and as 'King Kong' weighs in around 17 stones, his punch repaid it with interest and stretched out the guilty party. Delaye was immediately invited to join Audoubert in the changing-room. The final whistle signalled an all-out brawl. There was no security, so about 6,000 spectators invaded the pitch with the intention of helping out what few locals were left standing, while the Tricolors were leaving the field the legal way, with a police escort.

Queensland is the State of the gigantic. Everything is huge in what is essentially a farming area, and there are farms in the south as big as departements back home. The state itself is as big as France, England, Germany and Italy put together. It stretches more than 2,000 kilometres from north of Sydney to Cape York peninsula and nearly as far from the Pacific to the central desert. Barely two million live in this enormous expanse, 600,000 in the Brisbane conurbation alone, which prides itself on being the world's second biggest city, in area, after Los Angeles. 'Sunny Queensland' is a place to savour – the California of the southern hemisphere.

Visit its sun-kissed beaches famed for their 'sophistication' in importing every latest fad in bad taste and neon. There you'll find Surfers' Paradise with its girls galore, some gorgeous enough to sell your soul for and others so stupid you could weep. See the Great Barrier Reef with its wonderful necklace of islets, atolls and reefs stretching almost 3,000 kilometres from Bundaberg to Cape York.

Look round the plantations with their sugar-cane, pineapple and a whole range of other tropical fruits. Hunt crocodiles and learn the mysteries of boomerang throwing from the north's remaining aborigines. Don't make the mistake of killing harmless kangaroos which can block the road in hundreds. And don't be surprised if someone comes up and tries to sell you sheep, not just one but a whole flock! Finally, while Queensland is home to 200 million sheep, Queenslanders themselves are no little lambs, especially not on a rugby field. The Tricolors weren't long in finding that out.

After arriving in Brisbane, their first match was at the Gabba against the Queensland representative side. The Queensland selectors had gone for size. Nothing but great hulks: Duncan Hall, Brian Davies, Alan Thompson and Mick Crocker up front; MacCaffery, Flannery and Hazzard among the backs. To cap it all, an extraordinarily strong wind was blowing.

"A real mistral," joked Rinaldi from Marseilles.

But this mistral howled like a tornado behind Queensland. The tiniest of kicks and the ball flew like a shell towards the French posts. Not only that, but it hampered passing movements and stopped our forwards in their tracks. In the rear, miles behind, poor Puig-Aubert was struggling. His idea of training was one gentle lap of the pitch so now he couldn't draw breath, chasing after kicks with every gust of wind. To put it in a nutshell, the French pack wilted. Needless to say, this spiteful whirlwind blew defeat our way.

With the gale behind them, the Queenslanders mercilessly piled on the points. Poor 'flying Frenchmen'. They conceded two penalty goals to full-back Linde, a try to the big winger McGovern, converted by Linde, then one on the other wing to the athletic Flannery. What a great start. Not long after, scrum-half McCaffery scored another, again converted by Linde. Finally, right on half-time, fiery loose-forward Crocker bludgeoned his way over to extend the Queensland lead to 20-0.

The crowd was going mad. The popular side kept up a constant haunting chant of "Come on, Queensland." and how the Maroons responded. They had ripped France apart and it was going to be a monumental defeat. 20-0. Rugby is full of stories of comebacks, but no team had ever turned round such a deficit in a tourists match. In the second half, the wind would be behind them and it would be a different game, but could they overcome such a handicap? Queensland had defended ferociously as well as dominating in attack. Those who watched this famous match didn't appreciate at first the outrageous bravado of the French response.

They were awarded two penalties and Puig-Aubert launched two missiles from 50 metres out to trim Queensland's lead to 20-4. His sensational kicks won warm applause, but it was a bit like clapping a boxer who makes one last effort to get off the canvas and land a right-hander. This one-two in the face didn't faze Queensland who mounted an attack. Suddenly, a huge roar went up as Crespo leapt like a cat between big MacCaffery and huge Hazzard to intercept and dash under the sticks without a hand being laid on him. Pipette converted to make it 20-9 and, with half an hour left, a packed Gabba sensed that France were back in it. Confidence on the terraces had ebbed as France hit back. Nodding sagely, one fan might say, "You never know with these Frenchies". And his mate would snort, "Jeez, Johnny, be serious. They've got to score three more like that to win. Our lads will never let 'em in a million years."

The nagging doubt evaporated when Linde landed a difficult penalty against the wind to extend the Queensland lead to 22-9. Now the crowd relaxed, thinking the threat had passed.

"I told you, Johnny, we're the best team in Australia." He would have been absolutely right if Queensland had been playing New Zealand or Britain, but this was France. They were playing like demons and the scoreboard had hardly had time to register Linde's goal when Contrastin cut loose. Near his own line, he sent McGovern sprawling and sped almost the length of the field. His partner in crime, Cantoni, came sprinting across from the other wing, took the pass and went over by the posts. The conversion was a formality for Puig-Aubert and the Tricolors closed the gap to 8 points at 22-14. Another Puig-Aubert penalty cut the deficit still further and at 22-16, the stadium was no longer feeling so jubilant - anguished, more like. Every French move brought a gasp as the poor supporters had to endure an uncomfortable final quarter.

Making full use of his famous change of pace, Merquey raced clear with consummate ease and served his winger, Contrastin. 'Tintin' ploughed on and a worried crowd rose to its feet. Davies was just about to push him into touch when the Condom bruiser slipped an inside pass to Genoud who plunged over in the corner despite a desperate cover tackle by Linde. The gale came to

Queensland's aid and blew Puig-Aubert's conversion attempt off target - 22-19.

With only five minutes left, Queensland clung on to a lead which had melted like butter in a frying pan. Cling on, cling on at all costs was their only hope. France, however, had to take risks so, with just two minutes to go, Puig-Aubert launched a counterattack. Two sidesteps left burly props Hall and Thompson in his wake and he fed Merquey. Once again 'Jackie' cut through and found Contrastin on half-way. This was the final attack, their last hope. The crowd roared as if they believed their voices alone could hold Contrastin back or carry Linde into a tackle, but Linde, Queensland's last line of defence, was beaten. Contrastin had swept past him like a scrap of paper in the wind, but the Queenslander turned and chased, matching him stride for stride. Stubbornly, he refused to give up and allow Tintin to go behind the posts, forcing Contrastin to collapse right in the corner.

Puig-Aubert teed the ball up and struck it sweetly enough but again the gale diverted a kick which would have secured the win. But nothing, neither wind nor Queenslanders, could prevent the most incredible comeback in history. Down 20-0 at half-time and snatching a 22-22 draw, the word 'impossible' was obviously not in the French dictionary.

That night, the *Brisbane Telegraph* carried a full front page spread: "Brilliant France Superior. Frantic Finish to Exciting Draw".

France had two weeks before the second test, and two games to play in tropical north Queensland. These were against North Queensland, on 24 June at Townsville, well above the Tropic of Capricorn, and Wide Bay, at Bundaberg, on 27 June, three days before the test. The Tricolors enjoyed the break: bathing in the warm Coral Sea and visiting plantations of pineapple, paw paw, avocado and sugar cane. It was a holiday in paradise, which even the two scheduled matches could not spoil. Credit to the team, though, they concentrated on the job in hand and came up with two wins.

North Queensland had the reputation of being tough nuts to crack because the year before they'd given Great Britain a real game, but it proved false. France led 26-2 by half-time and won 50-17 without really extending themselves, with their try scorers being: Contrastin with three, Cantoni and Montrucolis two each, Comes, Crespo, Galaup, Bartoletti and Ponsinet. Pipette didn't seem to take it too seriously and only landed six goals, letting his mate, Comes, add a penalty. Three days later, at Bundaberg, common sense again prevailed and those chosen for the test were given a day off. With Montrucolis at centre and Galaup playing full-back, France dominated from beginning to end. Dop, injured in training the week before, enjoyed a run-out, our hero scoring one try and having a hand in the other nine by Maurice André with three, Martin with two, Bellan, Caillou, Rinaldi and Audoubert. With Caillou landing seven conversions, France ran out 44-19 winners.

With more than 100 points in the last two games, the atmosphere was euphoric. Everything was going well, too well, for there's nothing worse for a rugby team than overconfidence. And the Tricolors were indeed confident, especially once Dop and Brousse, who had suffered minor leg injuries in training for the Townsville game, were declared fit by their guardian angel, Australian masseur, Bill Moore.

Dop and Brousse were ready and Antoine Blain, Jean Duhau and so Bob Samatan announced only one change from the team which had won so sensationally in Sydney. Crespo had regained form and would play centre with Merquey moving to stand-off in place of Galaup. The team for the Gabba test was:

Puig-Aubert (captain); Contrastin, Crespo, Comes, Cantoni; Merquey, Dop; Mazon, Genoud, Bartoletti, Brousse, Ponsinet, Duffort.

The Gabba had the feverish atmosphere of a bullfight. It was not big enough to hold everyone who wanted to watch, with thousands travelling 400 or 500 kilometres overnight from the bush, often by truck. The Australian selectors had gone in for major surgery, the only survivor in the threequarters being the tough-as-teak 14 stones centre, Hazzard. Wingers Graves and Bliss had lost their places to the big, athletic Flannery and the smaller, lively Pidding who was the in-form kicker. The big centre Willoughby, butchered by Hazzard's crash tackling in the recent Queensland versus New South Wales match, was replaced by the stylish Geelan. Most radical of all, they had drafted in a new front-row with Duncan Hall paired at prop with tough fellow-Queenslander, Alan Thompson. At hooker, the selectors had ditched Schubert, not every Australian's first choice, in favour of Hammerton.

All in all, the Australian team had a more rugged look about it than the one which had lined up in Sydney. Motivated by a tremendous thirst for revenge, it would be backed by a crowd which clearly expected the Australian giant to wake from its slumber.

In a tense atmosphere that was not at all conducive to open rugby. Australia monopolised possession, taking a no-frills approach and keeping the ball tight. As the minutes ticked by, none of the expansive passing movements that had amazed the crowd in Sydney could develop. Wary of the dangers the French posed with their inspired attacking game, the Kangaroos played it safe.

For half an hour, the teams were locked in a violent arm-wrestle oblivious to everything around them. France led 6-4, but only because Puig-Aubert's boot was marginally more accurate than Pidding's. The Tricolors had made the mistake of thinking that they were bound to win, a confidence which was misplaced, for the Kangaroos, motivated as ever by a deep-rooted desire for revenge, scored twice before half-time. First Drew, the massive second-row, crashed through the French defensive line on the Australian 25. Prop Thompson carried the ball on into the French half, full-back Churchill came up in support and handed on to that remarkable opportunist, Holman, who scored between the posts. Pidding's conversion gave Australia a 9-6 lead.

Five minutes later, France suffered another hammer-blow. In a classic attack, Flannery broke free up the touchline and fed his supporting loose-forward, the blond Crocker. Pocket-battleship Crocker bumped off a tackler and passed to Hall who came on to the ball like a charging buffalo. Although his legs were held 15 yards from the line, he managed to slip the ball to Flannery who went over in the corner. "Australia 12 France 6", read the scoreboard at the end of the first half. Nevertheless the match wasn't over, for the Kangaroos were by now used to French comebacks and knew they would have to start the second half with exactly the same caution. The game fell into a rut of one-on-one battles and exchanges turned pretty rough as players took it out on each other, with punches coming in without warning. Most didn't know who'd hit them. Referee Tom McMahon had come to referee a rugby match and didn't really know what to do as the bad blood between players burst out in bouts of fighting.

The tide of nastiness carried Mr McMahon along with it, but dishing out penalties to keep the lid on it just wasn't enough to calm down overheated tempers. As players exchanged insults and settled old scores in the brawl, Merquey slipped away and the Australians were dismayed to see that he had the ball. Quicksilver Jackie raced off like a thief, and when the huge Drew blocked his path, he promptly passed to Cantoni who banged Drew off, leaving only Churchill to beat. Now Churchill harboured a profound dislike for Cantoni, perhaps because he had beaten him so many times, and went for him like a madman. Vincent put an astute little kick infield which rolled over the Australian line for Merquey to get there first. Puig-Aubert easily converted and the Australian lead was cut to 12-11.

First-aid men were kept busy on the touchline. Women had fits of hysterics in the stands and everyone howled disapproval every time Mr McMahon was brave enough to penalise a Kangaroo. It was so different from the sporting atmosphere of Sydney.

Among these little moments of 'overexcitement', one could appreciate in particular a punch by the fiery French scrum-half,

Dop. With a terrific right hook to the chin, he laid the chunky hooker Hammerton out cold... but two penalties against him allowed Pidding to put Australia back in control at 16-11.

Twice, three times, Merquey and Comes just failed to score but tempers were too inflamed, on the pitch and on the terraces, for handling movements to come to anything. As time went by a French defeat became more and more likely. It seemed certain 10 minutes from the end. Elie Brousse, that giant of a French second-row, whom Australia had tagged the 'Tiger of Sydney', had hands like shovels. He didn't tackle, he just laid a huge paw on an opponent's shoulder and the poor soul felt his knees give under the unbearable pressure. He would manage four or five yards then collapse at the Catalan's feet. The Australian, Hazzard, was one of the most amazing centres that we had ever seen: at 14 stones, with the legs and arms of a weightlifter, you don't see many like him. Elie Brousse's claw didn't bring him down at first, so the French superman seized him round the waist and smashed him to the ground. The Kangaroo line-breaker had never suffered such humiliation before and retaliated violently. They laid into each other only for Mr McMahon to send them both to the changing rooms where they had time to repeat to themselves, "I must not hit an opponent... under the referee's nose".

The loss of Brousse had a much greater effect on French morale than Hazzard's on Australia's. Without the great Elie, the French pack was bossed. Three minutes from time, the impressive prop, Duncan Hall, followed up a kick-ahead by scrum-half Holman to score close to the posts. The French hotly contested the try, claiming Hall had been offside, but it stood and the conversion by Pidding destroyed France's last hopes. On the final whistle, full-back Churchill put the icing on the cake with a 50-yard drop-goal and Australia had won 23-11.

The Gabba's red-hot atmosphere had been fatal, for it really got to France while galvanising an excellent Australian team. The Australian press acknowledged France's territorial superiority, but didn't hail the Kangaroo come-back with much enthusiasm: "This was the dirtiest international since the infamous Battle of Brisbane in 1922," wrote Jim Mathers in the *Daily Mirror*. A sickened Puig-Aubert told the *Sun*: "The Australians played the man and not the ball. They tackled us without the ball. Besides, they must have committed a fair number of fouls for Mr McMahon, despite the crowd's hostility, to have penalised them 11 times in the second half to France's six."

Harry Jefferies summed up perfectly the very special atmosphere of the battle of the Gabba in this article in the *Brisbane Telegraph:* "Australia Wins Amid Savage Scenes." And goes on:

"Women shriek hysterically, a French player bursts into tears under his own posts and the crowd roars, claps and throws paper into the air in delight as Duncan Hall smashed through the French defence to seal an Australian victory." Queensland is warm and Queenslanders are hot-blooded. Now the tour is beginning to look more like a crusade.

On 4 July, still in the state capital, France faced a stern test against a Brisbane Select. Tiredness meant the Tricolors had problems matching the tough home pack over 80 minutes, and the bell sounded with France trailing 16-15. In Australia, it isn't the referee who keeps time but a designated official, who signals full-time with a bell or a hooter and the referee must then blow up at the first stoppage. When the bell sounded, Brisbane rushed to make sure of victory by booting the ball out of play. But it didn't go out and Puig-Aubert, with an acrobatic leap, caught it out on the touchline where the two coaches, Jean Duhau and Bob Samatan, were packing up, faces gloomy in defeat.

"What shall I do?" Pipette shouted. "Oh, do what you want!" snorted Duhau. Two Australians had already singled out Puig-Aubert. He was in his own half, at least five yards from half-way and right on the touchline. Everything stopped in the ground. Spectators, who were previously on their way out, saw Pipette kick without even looking. The ball soared up and up and cleared the crossbar by a mile.

The crowd was stunned. Had it really happened? That wasn't a drop-goal, it was magic. With one fabulous kick, in the final seconds, Puig-Aubert had transformed certain defeat into a miracle win. Some spectators went on to the pitch to measure the legendary kick. It was precisely 60 yards from where Pipette had kicked to the try line and two yards in from touch. Fantastic!

France didn't leave Brisbane with happy memories. There had been the dramatic Queensland match in which they'd snatched a 22-22 draw after trailing 20-0 at half-time. A 23-11 defeat in the stormy second test and finally, the hard-won success over Brisbane. All this suggested a touch of weariness creeping in, but Queensland still had a nasty shock in store at Toowoomba, where the toughest rugby players came from, along with all sorts of other hard cases.

Toowoomba is the main town in an important farming region of Queensland's hinterland. The mountains round about were all volcanic and, before becoming extinct, fiery eruptions had piled up about 10 metres of ash which had created some of the richest agricultural land in the world. And it needed to be rich, for it had to nurture the best breeds of merino sheep as well as the burliest players in the southern hemisphere. Toowoomba, with a population of 40,000, is also the town which has supplied more players to the national team than anywhere apart from Sydney. By way of contrast Toowoomba doesn't provide the selectors with little lambs, but lads more like cowboys who enjoy a good Wild West saloon brawl. Currently, the team was led by Duncan Hall, the most fearsome prop on the continent and the man who had brought about France's defeat in the second test.

Right from the start, Hall had tried to intimidate Bartoletti, but he refused to let the Australian get on top and traded punch for punch. A little later, Hall was unhappy with a Brousse tackle and, like a tiger clawing, split Brousse's lip with a straight right. Elie replied with a left hook which left Hall chewing Toowoomba turf.

The referee exercised his authority and sent both off. Brousse left pointing to his injury but the crowd just chanted "We want Hall! We want Hall!" The game was stopped. Hall didn't want to go, so Bob Samatan signalled to Puig-Aubert to lead his men off. Straight away, police ringed the pitch. In the changing rooms, Antoine Blain and E.S. Brown, the Toowoomba president and a decent man, discussed the situation for a quarter of an hour. The French position was simple: two players were fighting, the referee had decided that both were to blame and had sent them off. As long as Hall stayed on the pitch, they, the French, would stay in their dressing room. Finally, Hall, the black sheep, was cajoled off the pitch back into the pen, and the game resumed with France in overall control, but still needing Pipette's boot to secure a 20-17 win.

The amiable Bill Corbett summed it up as follows in the next day's *Sun*: "Yesterday, in Toowoomba, I witnessed the most dramatic scenes."

The third test at the Sydney Cricket Ground in 1951

The triumphant French players sing the Marseillaise.

Enormous crowds wait for the SCG gates to open.
(Both courtesy Louis Bonnery)

Pipette beats Jim Sullivan

The Queensland part of the tour was over. Two days after the battle of Toowoomba, the Tricolors had to return to New South Wales and face North Coast at Lismore in a match which would be a red-letter day for Puig-Aubert. France won 33-9 and Pipette scored a try, four conversions and two penalties. At the end, the journalists all surrounded the full-back. "Well done. Well done."

"What's all the fuss about? I know I don't score many tries, but surely you don't need to make this song and dance." Pipette was astonished to learn that he'd just beaten the record for points scored on an international tour. It had been held by the florid, athletic Welshman, Jim Sullivan, a great full-back who had scored 132 points on the 1932 Great Britain tour. Puig-Aubert had amassed 133 and he wasn't finished yet.

Pipette returned to Sydney a living god. The Olympic Hotel was crammed with an endless stream of photographers, journalists and the merely curious, wanting to catch a glimpse of the French phenomenon who had just replaced the outstanding Jim Sullivan on the roll of honour. "You know, I didn't set out to break it. If I'd known anything about it, I'd probably never have beaten it," Puig-Aubert confessed to all the questions about how he'd gone about breaking the famous record.

Pipette was extremely modest. All his team-mates agreed that he would have been even more successful if he'd demanded to take every kick at goal and hadn't stepped down for some of the easy games. The following day, Pipette was really touched to receive a telegram all the way from Wigan: "Congratulations. Keep it going!" – signed: Jim Sullivan.

First there'd been the sensational game in Sydney, when a masterly Puig-Aubert goal snatched a 19-19 draw. Then the French uncorked their champagne rugby in the unforgettable 26-15 first test win. Now Sydney Cricket Ground was about to witness more history being made as France took on a New South Wales side which was probably just as strong as the full national team.

Only a week before a third test which would decide who were world champions, this game turned out to be incredibly intense. The fresher NSW team built up a 10-4 lead with tries from stand-off O'Connell, prop Brown and two Pidding goals. The Tricolors never looked like puncturing the home defence, but luckily they had the 'divine' Pipette. He succeeded with all his kicks, registering six penalties and a superb drop-goal to help France to a 14-12 lead with five minutes left.

But this tour, as we've said before, was no place for those with a weak heart. Fate had a nasty habit of only deciding the outcome at the very last moment. Beginning with the amazing France versus Sydney game on 2 June when Puig-Aubert snatched a 19-19 draw with the last kick of the match, we then had the sensational Queensland match on 15 June when the Tricolors came back from 20-0 down to sneak through right at the death with Contrastin's famous match-winner. Finally, there was the bruising Brisbane game when Puig-Aubert's phenomenal drop-goal after the bell pinched a 17-16 win. Surely enough last-minute miracles for anyone.

During this exceptional tour, fate had smiled on France with three wins at the death. So were the gods with us? Perhaps, but in the event, the referee awarded New South Wales a penalty just as the final whistle sounded and, from 30 yards out, Pidding put over the equalizing kick. 14-14.

Despite a praiseworthy effort by NSW, Australia only had eyes for Pipette. Breaking Sullivan's record had already put him on a pedestal, but keeping that great NSW team at bay with his magic boot, raised him to the pinnacle of fame.

Just like the first test, the crowd had poured into Sydney Cricket Ground the night before for the decider. £1 tickets to see the 'Flying Frenchmen' and 'Super' Puig-Aubert were going for £10 on the black market on the Thursday, and £20 on the morning of the match. The French camp had their problems. Hooker Martin was 50/50 with a knee injury and they were in two minds whether to pick Mazon 'The Terror' or reliable François Rinaldi at prop. Scrum-half Dop's absence through injury would disrupt the composition of the back-line, so it was only on the morning of the match that the officials came up with their final line-up:

Puig-Aubert (Captain); Cantoni, Comes, Merquey, Contrastin; Duffort, Crespo; Mazon, Genoud, Bartoletti, Brousse, Ponsinet, Calixte.

Dop's absence had necessitated a reshuffle, with Crespo moving to scrum-half and Merquey taking his place in the centres. Duffort switched to stand-off and Calixte came in at loose-forward. While these changes had been forced on them, the French selectors were confident that individual ability hadn't been sacrificed and that everyone would feel comfortable in his new position.

The biggest worry for Antoine Blain, Jean Duhau and Bob Samatan was what tactics the Kangaroos would use. They had learned a lot from coach Vic Hey's 'blitz' tactics in Brisbane. Get among them, don't let them settle and snap up every chance was all Australia seemed to offer. The violent second test had wound up the crowd and several incidents had marred it, but while the Tricolors' spectacular game had kept them on top, they had ultimately been thwarted by 13 big lads who were determined not to lose.

Was it going to be another physical confrontation? They feared so, for Australia had replaced the elegant Geelan at centre with the more direct Hawke, and at stand-off, a 'winner' in the shape of O'Connell came in for Stanmore. Prop Donoghue, a tough opponent, and hooker Schubert, a well-known hard player, were drafted back in for Thompson and Hammerton, both of whom were not considered rough enough. All four changes were made for the same reason: to put more steel into the Australian team. And anyway, Australian coach Vic Hey had been quite open about his tactics: "To beat France, you can't allow them any space at all."

All this worried the Australian Board of Control who dreaded a repeat of Brisbane. Some members feared the match might not even finish and president-elect George Ball felt he had to offer the following advice to the Australians the night before the game: "We want to make it very clear to every player that the reputation of rugby league is of paramount importance. Nothing must shame the sport we're all so proud to be involved with and none of you must stoop to illegal or dishonest tactics."

The press, too, leapt to a fervent defence of the way the French approached the game. Harry Jeffries, who had seen first-hand how Australian behaviour had worsened as the match went on, telephoned the *Brisbane Telegraph* on the eve of the test: "We want Australia to play by the rules against France and, if they do, France will win the series... Man-for-man, the French are superior. They are too fast, too enterprising."

France had won Australian hearts. The whole of Australia supported France as if the Tricolors were their own, and I've rarely known a whole nation feel such admiration and affection for a national team from abroad. Even today, I'm not sure what to admire more: the indisputable class of that French side or the warmth, enthusiasm and open friendliness of the great Australian sporting public.

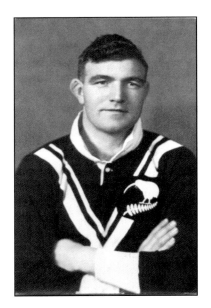

Jimmy Haig and George Menzies - both played for New Zealand against France in 1951. (Both courtesy Robert Gate)

The welcome home for the 1951 tourists in Marseilles.
(Courtesy Louis Bonnery)

Tricolor triumph

Sydney Cricket Ground was absolutely packed to the police limit. It felt like 14 July – Bastille Day - with the band in full scarlet tunics and colonial helmets and a crowd which had gathered the night before, or at dawn in the case of latecomers. But no, it was 21 July, a date to go down in history.

Despite those green jerseys, the crowd didn't have much confidence in the Kangaroos and you could have got 3/1 at one point. Polite applause greeted them but it was France the crowd were waiting for, and they came out of the tunnel to a tremendous roar. The setback at Brisbane had taught them a lesson and after Antoine Blain had laid down the law, they took the field determined to follow Duhau and Samatan's gameplan.

By this final stage of the tour, the French machine was tuned to perfection so changes made after Jean Dop's withdrawal shouldn't affect its smooth running. On the plus side, the players had shaken off the tiredness they had picked up in the middle of the Queensland section. This was the plan: really go for it from the first whistle. They had to catch the Kangaroos cold. Before kick-off, a little old man with grey hair went round the pitch to a reception fit for a king. It was Dally Messenger, 'The Master', the Australian idol from those old pioneering days. Despite the passage of time, he was still The Master and was there to shake the hand of the man who had come to take his throne. In front of a crowd of 92,000, he said he hoped Pipette would beat his records which had stood, seemingly unassailable, since 1910, the year in which Dally Messenger had landed 12 goals in the series against Great Britain.

In the first two tests, Puig-Aubert had totted up 11. Furthermore, during that 1910 tour, The Master had succeeded with 11 consecutive penalty goals while Pipette had, up until then, also managed 11 without missing. Both records were in danger and Messenger went back to his seat with the air of a man unhappy at losing something dear.

France stuck to their gameplan. From referee Tom McMahon's first whistle, the last of a long career, they tore into the attack in red, white and blue swarms. Puig-Aubert landed a second minute 40-yard penalty from wide out, then another just after. The Master had been mastered. Playing with incredible speed and without a single handling mistake, the Tricolors were simply inspired and swamped the Australians. Crespo made inroads on the right, Merquey and Comes created panic in the Australian defence, Contrastin raged like a wild beast all along the touchline and Brousse was more than ever the 'Sydney Tiger'.

When Puig-Aubert linked up with a dangerous attack by the backs, it created the space for Cantoni to gallop up the touchline, make 40 metres before turning it inside to the supporting Comes. He carried it on before feeding Crespo who sprinted under the posts. With Puig-Aubert's conversion, France went into a 9-0 lead after a quarter of an hour.

And the carnival continued. A break by the solid, yet subtle Duffort, 'René the Craftsman', and Jo Crespo was there to finish it off: 12-0. Not long after, a combined attack saw Contrastin plunge over triumphantly in the corner for 15-0. The Australian camp were beside themselves, and even two Pidding penalties didn't do much to raise morale. Their last hopes seemed to disappear when Brousse, who was having a tremendous game, got the ball 55 yards out, and launched himself on a wonderful run towards the Australian posts. He beat defenders for speed or brushed them off like feathers on an impressive charge to the line. The crowd rose in acclamation, then dropped to a murmur of "Brousse...Brousse," followed by enormous gasps of revulsion, indignation and fury. While Brousse was still stretched out by the post with the ball on the turf in front of him, all 15 stones of Davies crashed into him in pointless retaliation. Brousse's actual impact with the post wouldn't have been too bad if Davies hadn't caught Elie's head with his big boots as he slid in. Still groggy, the second-row was helped to the first-aid room and only really came to after half-time. While the crowd was still booing Davies, Puig-Aubert added the goal in his inimitable style and when the break came, France led 20-4.

Not long after the resumption, Duffort made another break and Crespo supported to surge over close enough to the posts for Pipette's conversion to be a formality. With a 25-4 lead, the Tricolors ran out of steam somewhat and the Kangaroos attacked near the line for Duncan Hall to bullock his way over. With Pidding's conversion, the score was looking a little more respectable at 25-9.

Again the French threequarters went on the offensive and Comes, with a couple of his trademark sidesteps, skipped over for a try easily improved by Puig-Aubert. Clearly, France were determined not to let slip a 30-9 lead. As the minutes ticked by, the Australian forwards continued with their one-dimensional tactic of simply driving the ball in until Davies managed to get over for Pidding to convert and bring the deficit back to 30-14.

France immediately counterattacked strongly and Contrastin went on the charge. Churchill made a brave attempt to stop him but 'Tintin' swatted him off and crashed over in the corner. Puig-Aubert's conversion meant France had triumphed, 35-14.

For the first time, France had scaled the heights. They were number one in the world, a feat no other French rugby team could match, even though, seven years earlier, the success of Lucien Mias's rugby union team in South Africa had heralded the arrival of French rugby on the world stage.

On Monday 23 July, *L'Equipe* carried the following headline: "Antipodes Shattered". Yes, people on the shores of the Pacific were shattered. Without a shadow of a doubt no French team has ever displayed similar qualities nor broken records like they did that day. It was the first time France had ever won a series against Australia which brought them the Tattersall Cup and the Goodwill Trophy, the latter a massive silver monument to bad taste, weighing more than 250 pounds. You could describe it as a supremely ugly First Communion cake but this was the trophy awarded to World Champions, to the team that had gained the best results at international level over a four-year cycle. Only four years after competition resumed after the war, France had gained the supreme honour in Sydney.

Yet another record went the Tricolors' way, that of highest score, for no other Australian team had ever conceded 35 points in a match. Their previous worst had come in 1910, a bad year when Great Britain had put 27 past them. Finally there were Puig-Aubert's feats, for that same day he had smashed Dally Messenger's record of 12 penalties and conversions in the 1910 series against Great Britain. Cheekily and with a touch of casualness, he had kicked 18 goals in the three tests. It would be difficult to beat his 50 per cent success rate while as for the overall tour points record set up by Jim Sullivan, Puig-Aubert had improved it from 132 to 161.

The whole stadium rose to the Tricolors on their lap of honour, Pipette carried aloft on their shoulders. "Well played, France!" the stands roared. The next day, under the headline,"Puig-Aubert smashes goal record in test triumph", Tom Goodman wrote in the *Sun-Herald*: "The third test at SCG yesterday was, yet again, an extraordinary triumph for that unforgettable star of French rugby: the little full-back, Puig-Aubert." Pipette was to gain huge popularity down under which is still as evident today. On my way home from the 1957 World Cup, a mechanical fault in the aircraft forced me into an extended stop-over in Darwin, in the tropical north. When the hotel's aboriginal porter found out I was interested in rugby, he pulled a scrap of paper out of his battered wallet. It was an old photo of Puig-Aubert kicking at goal.

After the third test, Pipette was the most popular man in Australia. You have to say it was as much for his good nature as his talent that he deservedly earned this reputation. Lovers of rugby ask today if we will ever see his like again. The international referee, Tom McMahon, who finished his career officiating in the three Australia versus France tests, claimed in the *Sun-Herald*:

"Puig-Aubert: Finest full-back in the world." He went on to say, "The Frenchman, Puig-Aubert, has been far and away the best full-back in the world over the last 25 years. Australians had always reserved that honour for their own Clive Churchill, but yesterday, Puig-Aubert completely dominated and outclassed Churchill. What's more, despite 21 years' experience as a referee, I've never been able to work out what he'd do next!"

Along with Pipette, Elie Brousse was another hero of the third test. That great forward of yesterday, Frank Burge, wrote of him thus in the *Sun-Herald*: "The Frenchman, Elie Brousse, is one of the greatest attacking forwards I have ever seen. His defence, too, has been tremendous in all three tests."

The formidable Jim Mathers, a cutting journalist who dipped his pen in vitriol more often than honey, stated in *Truth*: "Yesterday, our test team suffered their greatest-ever humiliation. France, who had come here as pupils to learn from the masters, wiped the floor with them at SCG and won the deciding third test by the irritatingly comfortable margin of 35-14. In the excitement of the match, a spectator, Mr John Wilson Dempsey of Islington, collapsed and died. Crushing prompted many spectators to try and get out of their sections. Some of the injured were detained in St Vincent's Hospital."

Finally, Alan Hulls in the *Daily Telegraph* reflected the opinion of most spectators, in writing: "To read the score, 35-14, is bad enough. It's worse to realise that this doesn't truly reflect the overwhelming superiority of the French."

There was uproar at the Olympic Hotel that night, for an excited crowd had accompanied the Tricolors to their headquarters. The owner, Jack Mason, emptied his whole stock of Champagne into the Tattersall Cup, which Puig-Aubert had carried back with him in triumph, leaving the French Rugby League with the job of transporting the World Championship "wedding-cake" home by boat, in a huge box two metres wide.

Until they left for New Zealand three days later, the French had a great time. After Champagne; Burgundy and Bordeaux had the honour of ending up in the Tattersall Cup from which everyone wanted a drink. Taxi drivers wouldn't take a penny from these Frenchmen nor would many souvenir shops. In short, our Tricolors were going to arrive in New Zealand on 25 July with haggard morning-after faces. "We'll all have eyes like piss-holes in the snow," Jean Duhau warned.

Their stay in New Zealand was meant to be a well-earned holiday, but this wasn't what the New Zealanders had in mind.

Under the leadership of Kupe, the first Maoris left Tahiti in their canoes in the 10th century. After several months at sea they sighted land, blanketed in dismal cloud, 700 kilometres away in the south-west. This North Island, however, turned out to be big, beautiful and welcoming with rich vegetation and animals which they may not have come across before, but at least were harmless. The Polynesian, Kupe, named the island Aotearoa or the Land of the Long White Cloud.

The French rugby league team only discovered Aotearoa in 1951, but they won't want to change Kupe's poetical description. If it's rain you want, the place to go is New Zealand. You can conjugate the verb 'to rain' every minute you're there. With this in mind, Old Rangi, a famous guide in the volcanic area of Rotorua, explained to me how the weather worked: "When you can see the mountains, it's going to rain."

"And when you can't see them?"

"It's already raining!"

What with rain, pitches which are mudheaps, one-eyed referees who only spot infringements by visitors, exhaustion after three months of touring and the after-effects of partying following their third test triumph, the Tricolors badly needed breathing space. Given these circumstances, it was extraordinary how they went about defending their reputation. After disembarking on South Island, they beat West Coast 5-2 at Greymouth but lost Delaye with a shoulder problem. At Christchurch they overcame South Island 13-7, but Comes injured an ankle. On their way back to Auckland, the economic hub, they stopped off in Wellington where they won again, 26-13.

Carlaw Park in Auckland has never been the Tricolors' favourite venue, for there's no bigger quagmire anywhere and, being at sea-level, water can't drain away. It's strange to see a flock of seagulls foraging for tit-bits in the muddy earth while a game goes on in another part of the field. On a swamp like this, the Tricolors were never able to turn on the style because they couldn't employ their main strike weapon – speed. Then there's the unbelievable level of suspicion that referees in New Zealand harbour towards teams from abroad. I've seen referees there award five times as many penalties against France as the locals. In the only test played, M.J. Griffin was par for the course and, even today, Puig-Aubert will tell you that he thought he was 'bent'.

"Sure he was," Pipette claimed after the match. "The best player on the Kiwi side was Mr Griffin. He disallowed three tries, one of which, Brousse's, was nailed-on. And anyway, he'd actually given it and I was preparing to take the conversion, when Robertson, the New Zealand centre and captain, came and complained that there'd been a forward pass by Cantoni to Brousse. Mr Griffin disallowed

Puig Aubert complains about Martin's sending off in Auckland.
(Courtesy Louis Bonnery)

the try. A little later he sent off our hooker Martin. Then, in the last minute, while we were leading 15-14, he penalised us. White kicked the goal and we lost 16-15. And yes, I do harbour a grudge against Mr Griffin!"

Pipette had missed the first few matches in New Zealand after having a wisdom tooth extracted, but saw the Tricolors go on to avenge the test defeat two days later by beating an Auckland side which contained nine internationals. France generally controlled the match, winning 15-10 after leading 15-2 with five minutes to go. To complete the visit, France crushed South Auckland 25-7 and, in New Plymouth, Taranaki 23-7.

On their return to Wellington, the French party were touched by the warmth of their welcome by the Queen of the Maoris. With garlands round their necks, they listened spellbound to choirs which sang a mixture of war-like hakas and love ballads. It was a well-earned rest. When they got back to the hotel, Antoine Blain announced that Australia wanted to save pride by playing a fourth test. They'd be taking a big gamble in going along with the request, for the team was washed out, whereas the Kangaroos would doubtless have trained hard to restore their reputation. To turn it down would be contrary to their chivalrous spirit so, after talking it over with Jean Duhau, Bob Samatan and the players, Antoine Blain sent a telegram accepting.

This unscheduled fourth test was marked down for 18 August in Melbourne. Antoine Blain and the coaches, Jean Duhau and Bob Samatan, were clearly very worried. Props Bartoletti, Mazon and Rinaldi were all unfit. Scrum-half Dop, too, was unavailable as well as stand-offs Duffort and Merquey. Centre Comes and wingers Cantoni and Lespès had also pulled out. On the plus side, the tour party enjoyed strength in depth and those regarded as reserves often performed just as well in the French jersey as the first choices. The three men in charge came up with this patched-up team:

Puig-Aubert (captain); Maurice André, Caillou, Crespo, Contrastin; Bellan, Calixte; Beraud, Martin, Audoubert, Brousse, Ponsinet, Perez.

Just reading through this line-up shows how tricky it had been to get a side together. Maurice André, who usually played full-back, was on the wing; elegant loose-forward Calixte was down to play scrum-half and Audoubert, later to make a name for himself as an outstanding hooker, was moved up to prop. Before agreeing to play it, Antoine Blain had insisted that this test would be regarded as unofficial. The Australians pulled their faces, disappointed that they couldn't use the game to put the record straight, but accepted with good grace.

While the bulk of the party, led by Antoine Blain and Bob Samatan, boarded the Stratheden bound for Marseilles, those picked for the game flew to Melbourne with Jean Duhau. They would pick up the Stratheden later in Adelaide.

The normally cheerful Puig-Aubert was the only worried man on the plane. He had important decisions to make, for Sydney St George, the richest club in Australia, had offered him a three-year contract worth eight million francs plus 100,000 per month, a detached house and return tickets for his wife and little girl. It was all very well being a world star, but Puig-Aubert, though content, wasn't a wealthy man. He had asked for three days to think it over, and that was what he was doing.

Eager to board ship for home, the Tricolors briskly completed their Melbourne business. They quickly found their best form and were so superior to the Kangaroos that the film of the match is kept in the ARL archives and still brought out for Australian coaches to study.

In crushing Australia again, this time by 34-17, Beraud scored two and Maurice André, Crespo and Contrastin one each. But the game's outstanding personality was Puig-Aubert who amassed 19 points with four penalties, four conversions and, for good measure, a try. This time, you couldn't put it down to a temporary Australian loss of form. The following day's *Melbourne Morning Herald* led with "Brilliant champagne rugby too much for Kangaroos".

Jacques Merquey in action against the Kiwis.
(Courtesy Louis Bonnery)

As for Puig-Aubert, he had become a god. In the Sydney *Daily Mirror*, Arthur Mailey wrote: "Puig-Aubert may have collected souvenirs for his sports shop but I'm willing to bet that the best thing for this great player to take back home with him is a set of goalposts. When he places the ball for a kick, he about-turns, glances up at the clock and natters with the reserves on the touchline. I'm sure he could kick one from the dressing rooms if he was sure the officials weren't frightened of getting hit on the back of the head."

The whole of Australia lay at his feet and he was very tempted to take the gold it offered. He had another meeting with the St George directors arranged for Monday 22 August, just before Jean Duhau's party caught up with the Stratheden in Adelaide. The evening before, he was intending to stay on. "After all, three years will soon pass," he told his mates. He was meeting the directors the following day at lunch time. When he woke up, he was a bag of nerves. His room-mate, Contrastin, was packing his bag.

"Now, Pipette, OK if I leave?"

"Fine," he replied, dragging on his first cigarette of the day. The little group met in the hall, but Pipette didn't say a word. He wanted to crack a joke to banish the gloom that hung over his team-mates, but was frightened the words would stick in his throat. Jean Duhau, who had never just been a coach but father, brother and trusted friend to his players, gnawed at a nail, eyes glued to the floor. When he eventually lifted his head, his eyes met Pipette's. In those sad eyes, Pipette saw all the warmth that he would miss for three years.

When the St George directors arrived, the Tricolors moved out of the way. Were they going to lose Pipette? His gut reaction was that if he stayed, it would be like losing a part of his life, so politely but firmly, he declined the offer. The Australians shook hands, wished him bon voyage, waved goodbye to the team and left.

Straightaway the Tricolors crowded round Pipette who said rather emotionally in that hoarse voice of his: "Yeah, I've weighed it up. I thought with you gone, and no Gauloises and pastis, how could I train? No, it's an act of God that's making me go home."

They left on the Stratheden, happily and with a full complement, and stopping off at Perth, their last port of call in Australia, hammered Western Australia 70-23. By notching up 20 points – seven goals and two tries – Puig-Aubert beat Jim Sullivan's overall points record of 223 for a tour of Australasia. His total came to 236 points: 106 penalties, drop-goals and conversions and eight tries.

Australia was left stunned by the lack of inhibition in France's rugby; a novel approach to the game. To become a champion in the antipodes, one has to make a total commitment. Serious training, diet and abstinence are the principles on which success is based in Australia. Then France came. No respecters of convention, they overturned all the theories of the fitness experts, so much so that the *Sydney Morning Herald* launched an inquiry: "After seeing French speed and liveliness, one has to doubt the efficacy of the régimes put together by our sports experts. These quick and intelligent players have thrown all the dieticians into a panic with the huge quantities of bread they consume. Waitresses in the hotel spent most of their time bringing more bread. On top of that, they drink as much table wine every day as we could manage at a former servicemen's dinner – and they don't stint themselves on beer either. They are particularly fond of mashed potatoes. Most of them smoke. And again, they have a peculiar habit of pouring a big glass of red wine into the dregs of their soup, which seems to cheer everyone up enormously. All this might make our coaches frown, but look at the results. These French have outclassed us."

The following day, a dietician responded, "It's a real shame that

The triumphant lap of honour after the third test victory at the
Sydney Cricket Ground. (Courtesy Louis Bonnery)

the nutritional standards of the famous French team have been
so poor. If they had followed our basic sporting diet sheets and
avoided certain dishes and drinks, they would have been even
more formidable."

The *Sydney Morning Herald*, however, remained unconvinced by
this argument and suggested the following day: "The full-back,
Puig-Aubert, is an absolute marvel. Why, he smokes like a chimney,
quaffs everything he can and has an absolute horror of training!"

Overall, the dieticians were probably right. By ignoring any
nutritional régime and avoiding any serious training, the
phenomenon that is our Pipette quickly grew globe-shaped and as
he himself laughed: "I've developed such stomach muscles I can't
see my shoes any more!"

He continued to do the impossible for several more years, still
smoking two packs of Gauloises, drinking 12 or more pastis a day
but, most importantly, scrupulously refraining from any training. He
still performed miracles but, as Jean Duhau said, what could he not
have achieved if "he had not overdone the kick-and chase?"

But when all's said and done, the character and charm of rugby
lies in enjoying it. Evidently, the passage home on the P&O's
Stratheden was a very happy one. The passengers hadn't time to
get bored. Those known as 'The nutcases' for their loud laughter
(Puig-Aubert, Mazon, Martin, Ponsinet, Contrastin, Lespes and
Bartoletti) let their hair down. People fell in the pool, firecrackers
went off in the dining room and Antoine Blain, for all his authority,

couldn't cope. One day, the captain invited him to the bar for a scotch. Perched on stools, they chatted amicably and enjoyed their whisky. The ship's captain, a real gentleman, spoke thus to Antoine Blain, gaining himself the nickname of 'the lawyer' from the Carcassonne contingent: "Mr Blain, your lads are very nice, but they make too much noise. Yesterday, we had three firecrackers go off. It is a little too..." Here, Antoine Blain tried to excuse our rowdy boyos. "What do you want them to do, captain? They're young, they've just been hailed world champions, so these are really just explosions of joy. I'll go and talk to them and I assure you they'll be good from now on..."

Antoine Blain had hardly finished talking when a huge firecracker exploded under the captain's stool and even he had to burst out laughing. Their arrival in Marseilles on 19 September was a veritable triumph. Each in his own decorated car, the 'Australians' paraded through the Old Port and the Canebière, between ranks of spectators 10 deep. Such a sight had never been seen before... even in Marseilles.

Paul Barrière and Claude Devernois were waiting on the quay amid a sea of spectators and an army of reporters, photographers and film crews. This carnival in Marseilles, with so many flags and so much bunting, was like Liberation Day all over again. Every player, a garland round his neck, stood up in his very own convertible at the front of which you could see his name in huge letters. It was like a Broadway parade and so that tens of thousands of Marseillais could hail their heroes, all traffic had been stopped in the Old Port, the Canebière, the Gambetta alleés, the rue de Rome, and the cours Belsance. With a police escort and showers of paper tricoloured cockerels, banners stretched across the Canebière read "Glory to the French Rugby League team", "Hail the Tricolors". For the French team, the Orient Gate had become the Golden Gate.

Wasn't this just reward for those who had set off, alone and unappreciated, amid a nation's indifference?

The programme from the first test of the 1955 tour.

III. 1955: A coronation down under

"My centre is giving way, my right is in retreat; situation excellent, I shall attack..."
Marshal Foch

When it was time for him to retire, Lolo Mazon was offered a parting gift by the Carcassonne club. 'Grandad Taillefer', as he was known, was the owner of a hooter which had suffered greatly from scrums and squabbles. In return for his loyal service, they offered to make it like a Greek god's and, thanks to the plastic surgeon's expertise, the operation was a complete success. If his blond hair hadn't been even more difficult to manage than its owner, he could easily have been taken for the Kirk Douglas of Languedoc. Unfortunately, destiny decided to thumb her nose at him.

One fine Sunday morning, the famous Carcassonne club found itself short of a big prop. The supporters went off in search of Lolo to see whether he'd do this little favour. Good grief, one game wouldn't make any difference to an old warrior, and anyway, the bugger was still in good nick. On principle, he made them beg a bit, maybe with a small consideration also in mind. They reminded him how Carcassonne had won everlasting glory in Championship and Cup. The pride of Occitania must be preserved! Surely he wasn't going to let Villeneuve, Albi, Bordeaux, Lyons, Marseilles or the Catalans come and lay the law down in full view of the Cité? Hearing this, Lolo decided to enter the arena once more.

So he returned to the front line, his classical profile a rallying point. His comeback was going superbly, when a minor skirmish suddenly broke out. The Carcassonne trainer was called for and Lolo left the field with a bloody nose. And this is why today, thanks to unkind fate and an opponent's fist, this prop Mazon, nicknamed 'The wild man' in the antipodes, sports a nose which exemplifies his whole career: expressive, tortured and belligerent. Nothing frightened him, player, crowd or referee, except the displeasure of his charming wife who led him, shall we say, by the nose.

After Grandad Taillefer, 'Uncle Edouard' was the next to announce the end of his international career. No doubt Edouard Ponsinet would continue to crack nuts in the crook of his arm or open a tin of sardines without a key, just pulling with thumb and forefinger on the little metal tongue, but this gentle giant had made his family the priority, and contented himself with coaching the new generation in Lezignan.

Even the clerk at the local railway station got in on the act, greeting arrivals with barely disguised menace: "Lézignan. End of the line". And for many teams it was.

Without these two stalwarts, the Carcassonne fans couldn't come out with their favourite song any more, to the tune of *Vive le Vent*:

"Un essai de Ponsinet
Vive l'ASC
Un second
De Mazon
Ah! Le bon garcon!"

Martin Martin, called 'The Spaniard' because he'd been born in Valladolid, and Henri Vaslin, nicknamed 'The Austrian' because of his blond hair, also made themselves unavailable for international selection. All too soon, Vincent Cantoni with an injured knee and Elie Brousse with a ruptured Achilles tendon followed suit. Beraud, heavily involved in Avignon's recovery and the growth of his café business, and good old Raoul Perez, 'The Gipsy', who had become less and less interested in training, stepped out of the limelight. 'Organiser' Calixte, too, suffered a knee injury and hung up his boots. Caillou and Comes both left quietly while still at the top. René 'The craftsman' Duffort, after a spell as captain-coach of Paris Celtic, quit to swell the ranks of café owners. Finally, president Barrière left the stage after the 1954 World Cup to pursue his passion for bullfighting.

While international players continued to say their goodbyes, Claude Devernois remained the motive force behind the 'new' rugby. Although the French team had lost quite a few of their 'Australians', they continued to play well and managed victories against New Zealand and Australia who toured in 1951-52 and 1952-53. More wins came in the World Cup, against New Zealand in Paris and Australia in Nantes, but they could only manage a draw against Great Britain. They reached the final in Paris only to go down narrowly 16-12 to the British.

When the time came for the second campaign in Australia, some of the 1951 heroes were still willing to tour: Puig-Aubert, despite his priestly paunch; Dop, who had not yet settled down; Merquey, still as good as ever; 'Dumbo' Delaye, who cheerfully weighed in at well over 15 stones; Montrucolis, an old lion who could still raise a roar; the influential 'Monseigneur' Audoubert and Contrastin, who may have lost a little pace, but still knew the way to the line.

To this core of experience, one could add young guns and one near-ancient in Gabriel Berthomieu, nick-named 'Hugues' quite simply because for the first post-war game against England, on 23

February 1946 at Swinton, in alphabetical order he was the first 'cap'. It wasn't much of a jump to make the connection with Hugues Capet, the first king of that line. Before they left for this second tour, the Tricolors suffered their first setback. Puig-Aubert injured his left arm in the third minute of the cup semi-final at Lyons on 24 April. He was taken to the Edouard-Herriot Hospital where it was found that he had fractured his humerus. His tour as French captain was over and there was dismay both in France and down under, where everyone wanted to see the incomparable Pipette again. For France, it was a disaster, for no other full-back could compare, nor was there any one on the horizon to succeed a player voted 'Champion of Champions 1951' by *L'Equipe.*

On Saturday 7 May, the selectors met in Marseilles to pick the party to play 25 matches in Australia and eight in New Zealand. The four month tour would be led by Antoine Blain with Jean Duhau and René Duffort as coaches and these 28 players:

Full-backs: Dop (Marseilles), G. Benausse (Carcassonne).
Wingers: Contrastin and Ducasse (Bordeaux), Savonne (Avignon), Voron (Lyons), F. Cantoni (Toulouse).
Centres: Merquey (Avignon), Teisseire (Carcassonne), Rey and Larroudé (Lyons).
Stand-offs: Jiminez (Villeneuve), Delpoux (Carcassonne).
Scrum-halves: Guilhem (Carcassonne), Menichelli (Paris Celtic).
Props: Vanel (Lyons), Berthomieu (Albi), Fabre (Avignon), Carrère (Villeneuve).
Hookers: Audoubert (Lyons), Moulis (XIII Catalan).
Second-rows: Montrucolis (Cavaillon), Pambrun and Delaye (Marseilles), Save (Bordeaux), Jammes (Carcassonne).
Loose-forwards: Duplé (Bordeaux), Levy (XIII Catalan).

Obviously, some areas were not fully filled, because each player could cover several positions. The last member of the party was a supporter, Roland Proust, the Parisian referee.

The first of the two groups to leave, led by Blain and Duhau, had to fulfil the first fixtures until the rest joined them in Sydney a week later. There were 17 in this advance guard: Dop, Ducasse, Contrastin, Savonne, Cantoni, Jiminez, Larroudé, Duplé, Menichelli, Levy, Save, Pambrun, Delaye, Carrère, Moulis, Berthomieu and Fabre. Well before the French team had been picked, Australian supporters had besieged the ticket offices. When the small French party reached Darwin on Friday 13 May, you couldn't get a ticket for the first test on 11 June for love nor money.

Pen-pictures of the 1955 tour party

1. Jacques Merquey (Avignon) (Captain). Centre. 10 stone 8 pounds; 5 feet 5 inches; 25; Chemist. Undoubtedly one of the cleverest attacking centres in the game. He has a sharp burst of speed which enables him to flash through the smallest of gaps. He is an expert at the interception and is, in all respects, a constant danger. Fine tackler.

2. Gabriel Berthomieu (Albi) Second-row. 14 stone 3 pounds; 5 feet 10 inches; 31; Truck driver. Solid performer who takes the ball up well. A forward who would never let you down, he inspires those around him and tackles with ferocity. Very keen on crocodile hunting.

3. Maurice Voron (Lyons) Winger. 11 stone 11 pounds; 5 feet 9 inches; 26; Designer. Extremely dangerous on attack – fast and intelligent. Came over to rugby from athletics, and has made rapid progress under René Loste.

4. Fernand Cantoni (Toulouse) Winger. 12 stone 4 pounds; 5 feet 10 inches; 22; Clerk. Brother of Vincent who toured in 1951. Probably the fastest player in the party, he is an accomplished finisher who is improving with every game.

5. André Ducasse (Bordeaux) Winger. 11 stone; 5 feet 6 inches; 25; Transport worker. Compact winger whose clever dodging runs have made him a great favourite with the crowds. Not over-fast, but times his runs well. Loves to kick ahead.

6. André Savonne (Avignon) Winger. 11 stone 12 pounds; 5 feet 6 inches; 24; Clerk. Pacy winger who uses his build to advantage, enjoying physical assets which enabled him to replace the elder Cantoni. Shows so much power, he has been nicknamed 'The Bison', but owes much to the great Avignon coach, Beraud.

7. Raymond Contrastin (Bordeaux) Winger. 12 stone 4 pounds; 5 feet 8 inches; 30; Clerk. Perhaps not as sprightly as four years ago, but is still a determined runner and expert at cutting infield for the inside pass. Often argues on-field with Dop. Had a great World Cup and forms the 'mad club' with Carrère.

8. Claude Teisseire (Carcassonne) Half-back or centre. 11 stone; 5 feet 4 inches; 24; Mechanic. A little man with a big reputation. He is all class, but has the heart to go with it. Never gives up and dodges big men with ease. A real match-winner whose low tackling is amazing. Likes to 'wind up' opponents.

9. Roger Rey (Lyons) Centre. 11 stone; 5 feet 11 inches; 24; Driver or mechanic. Straight, hard runner who prefers to go over rather than round. One of the soundest and most reliable in the party. No slouch on attack. Suffered from a knee injury in 1954-55, but is now fully recovered.

10. Victor Larroudé (Lyons) Centre. 11 stone 9 pounds; 5 feet 6 inches; 24; Clerk. This René Duffort discovery has made sensational progress – eight months before the tour, he hadn't played rugby. Now his speed and awareness have propelled him into the touring party. Has the confidence of the selectors.

11. Gilbert Benausse (Carcassonne) Full-back. 12 stone 8 pounds; 5 feet 9 inches; 23; Hairdresser. Began as Puig-Aubert's replacement, but after a shaky start, he found his feet and showed he is a first-class footballer. Neat and quick to back up, he is a fine goalkicker and is currently the leading points scorer with well over 100. Coach Félix Bergèse reckons he will develop into a fine loose-forward.

12. André Delpoux (Carcassonne) Stand-off. 11 stone; 5 feet 7 inches; 27; Vigneron. He played his first two seasons at Carcassonne as an amateur. His pace and solid defence have made him a superb utility player.

13. Antoine Jiminez (Villeneuve) Stand-off. 11 stone 12 pounds; 5 feet 6 inches; 26; Schoolteacher. So impressed with the reports of games and the reception the returning 1951 tourists received, he changed codes. A wonderful handler, he is regarded as one of the finest French players of the day. Very keen educationalist.

14. Jean Dop (Marseilles) Half-back or full-back. 11 stone 11 pounds; 5 feet 5 inches; Café proprietor. Fantastically talented, but very erratic. Never short of a word on or off the field. Can win a match or lose it, but one has to admire his daring. A comedian. Now captain-coach at his beloved Marseilles, "Jeannot" is a one-off.

15. Sylvain Menichelli (Paris Celtic) Scrum-half. 11 stone; 5 feet 7 inches; 27; Commercial traveller. 'Mic' is strong, skilful and a past master at sneaking through tight defences. Sometimes too flamboyant, but isn't that the French way?

16. François Montrucolis (Cavaillon) Loose-forward. 14 stone 5 pounds; 5 feet 10 inches; 32; Café proprietor. Not a spectacular player, but one of those grafters that every team needs. Happy mixing it in any company. Mud will not put this man off.

17. Guy Delaye (Marseilles) Prop. 17 stone; 6 feet 1 inch. A bad shoulder injury on the 1951 tour nearly ended his career. The biggest member of the party, but by no means overweight and is in fine playing condition. Very difficult to stop, he takes the team forward and grafts solidly. Has fully recovered from a World Cup knee injury.

18. Jean Pambrun (Marseilles) Second-row. 15 stone; 5 feet 11 inches; 25; Pastry cook. Seems to have modelled his game on Ponsinet – even down to wearing similar headgear. Very dangerous runner out wide. Played on with two broken fingers in the World Cup Final and had to wear a brace for two months after.

19. Armand Save (Bordeaux) Second-row. 13 stone 7 pounds; 5 feet 7 inches; 23; Butcher. Developed rapidly under coach Duhau, has added a few pounds, and become renowned for his vitality and punch. Off the field, he is quiet and shy. A real Pyrenean mountain boy.

21. Jacques Fabre (Avignon) Prop. 12 stone 13 pounds; 5 feet 9 inches; 26; Company director. Grafting type of forward who can always be relied on to do his bit. A lot of his work could be overlooked, but the coaches think highly of him.

22. Jean Jammes (Carcassonne) Second-row. 15 stone 4 pounds; 5 feet 9 inches; 26; Company director. Powerful forward who can play on the wing because of his searing pace. He needs more big-match experience.

23. Joseph Vanel (Lyons) Prop. 13 stone 7 pounds; 5 feet 11 inches; 28; Slaughterman. A very consistent performer who runs hard for the full game. It is a mistake to stand off him – he will take advantage. A real asset to a tour party.

24. André Carrère (Villeneuve) Hooker. 14 stone 5 pounds; 5 feet 10 inches; 31; Commercial representative. Magnificently built, with prodigious strength and astonishing speed, he is an expert at beating the strongest defence. Enjoys an argument.

25. Jean Audoubert (Lyons) Prop. 15 stone 2 pounds; 5 feet 10 inches; 31; Storekeeper. 'Dou-dou' is not exactly svelte, but surprisingly fast and undeniably powerful. Very competitive, his attitude inspires his colleagues.

26. René Moulis (XIII Catalan) Hooker. 13 stone 5 pounds; 5 feet 8 inches; 23; Carpenter. Under the tutelage of René Duffort, he has quickly became one of France's best hookers. Solid, with fine technique.

28. Francis Levy (XIII Catalan) Centre. 11 stone 9 pounds; 5 feet 7 inches; 24; Designer. Solidly built, speedy and determined, he is a 'jack of all trades' for Catalans. Played with Puig-Aubert, Brousse and Duffort at Paris Celtic.

29. Roger Guilhem (Carcassonne) Loose-forward. 11 stone 13 pounds; 5 feet 8 inches; 29; Butcher. Alternating at international level between scrum-half and loose-forward, his extraordinary tackling ability earned him the nickname of 'Octopus'. Is fully fit for the tour after an injury-hit World Cup.

30. Christian Duplé (Bordeaux) Loose-forward. 13 stone 1 pound; 5 feet 11 inches; 25; Company manager. A fine attacking forward who works well with his scrum-half. Always on the alert for openings, he is also a crafty passer of the ball. Excellent goalkicker.

Antoine Blain (Manager; secretary-general, FFR XIII) One of the pillars of French rugby league since 1937. Captured by the Nazis during the war, but escaped. Enjoyed one post-war season as a player, then switched to coaching with the great Carcassonne team. Managed the 1951 team.

Jean Duhau (Bordeaux) Coach. Played right up to the outbreak of war, having been one of 'Galia's Boys' in 1934. Big Jean is quietly-spoken and less excitable than many of his countrymen. The ideal coach, he played in every position in the pack. Toured in 1951.

René Duffort (Lyons) Coach. The youngest of France's 'Big Three', he still plays in France, but is on tour solely in a coaching capacity. A smart and successful player in 1951, and a shrewd reader of a game.

The tour started with a victory in Perth on 15 May against Western Australia, a huge territory six times as big as France. Under a Riviera sky, the attendance record was broken. In 1951, 7,000 fans came to see the French triumph 70-23, but this time the crowd was 15,200. Western Australia had improved their defence considerably and were only beaten 31-6. It's worth noting that the Bordeaux contingent scored all the points with three tries each from Contrastin and Save, two from Ducasse, while Duplé scored a try and kicked two goals.

On Wednesday 18 May, the Tricolors really turned on the cavalier style at the expense of South Australia. On top form, they won 48-10 and prompted the *United Press Agency* to cable: "Speed, skill, snappy passing. Crowd seemed absolutely stupefied. Not used to such spectacular play."

France ran up the trifling total of 12 tries: Savonne and Fernand Cantoni three apiece, Dop with two, while Jiminez, Carrere, Moulis and Duplé scored one each. Continuing their run of victories, they destroyed Victoria 44-2 in Melbourne on Saturday, 21 May. Again they crossed for 12 tries with two each from Ducasse, Larroudé, Moulis and Duplé and one each to Jiminez, Contrastin, Delaye, and Save. France returned to the federal capital, Canberra, with the very impressive points-for total of 123. Too impressive perhaps, for Monaro Division thought they could dish some treatment out to opponents tired out by a long voyage and three games in six days. The Tricolors felt they had something to offer in this area too, so a free-for-all broke out. Police had to step in to calm the crowd. The referee had obviously made up his mind not to saddle himself with complicated decisions about right and wrong, but following King Solomon's example, sent off Australian Moon and Frenchman Moulis. The match ended in relative calm, but France were beaten for the first time, 11-3. This hadn't come about by accident. Illusions had taken hold, for wins had come so easily they had let themselves slip into the nasty habit of not playing as a team. They were absolutely buried by a strong Sydney side in the kind of quagmire all French teams hate. 25-0. Unbelievable.

Thankfully, reinforcements arrived in the shape of René Duffort and his mini-army of 11 who, before leaving, had taken time out to wallop Wales 24-11 in Nantes. They were: Audoubert, Vanel, Jammes, Montrucolis, Guilhem, Voron, Rey, Delpoux, Teisseire, Merquey and Gilbert Benausse.

Three days later in Narrandera, no doubt inspired by Sydney, Riverina played such an aggressive game that two of them, Alan Staunton and Jack Slavin, were banned for a year. France, however, lost the game 29-27 and had Jammes taken to hospital.

The improvement shown in Narrandera continued on the following Saturday 4 June, when they faced New South Wales in Sydney. As usual, France put on a marvellous performance at the Sydney Cricket Ground and even though they were effectively reduced to 12 men after Berthomieu suffered a broken hand in the first few minutes, they played superbly. Their speed, awareness and ability to switch play meant that after trailing 22-18 only 14 minutes from the end, they clawed back to 24-24 with only two minutes left.

Then came the decisive moment of the match. Under pressure on their own line, the French tried to break out and protect the draw. You only had to hear the crowd shouting for them to know they were still Sydney's favourite sons. The injured Berthomieu, who had insisted on staying on the field, got the ball but couldn't pass with his broken hand. A big tough lad, this 'Hugues' of ours, and so ignoring the pain, he took it in, making one, 10, 20 yards. The crowd rose to his sacrifice but saw the bald prop, Roy Bull, smash into him. Any other time, Berthomieu wouldn't have batted an eyelid, and I was reminded of a confession he made to me after the French win over Great Britain at Parc des Princes earlier the same year: "I had difficulty breathing during the game. I must have had a cold."

A week later, Dr Bonpunt revealed that Berthomieu had difficulty breathing because he had two broken ribs! That day, however, he lost the ball as Bull crashed into him with tremendous force. The international stand-off, Darcy Henry, picked it up and went under the posts. Cruelly, unjustly, France lost 29-24. After the disappointment against Sydney, this narrow, some would say undeserved, defeat by NSW made the Australian public feel better, for they were pleased to see their old 'Unpredictable Frenchmen' back again. It had been a lively match played out in a good spirit, the sort that demonstrates a rapport between crowd and players. A game like this seems to transform mere mortals into knights of old like Lancelot or Parsifal. The *Sun-Herald* headlined: "Champagne again" but France weren't happy; knowing only too well there were worrying flaws and faults. The injury to Berthomieu didn't help matters either. Brave Berthomieu had discovered a new lease of life when he had gone crocodile hunting in Chad the year before – for six months. His legendary courage and reputation as an experienced international inspired the young Tricolors and sowed the seeds of doubt among the battle-hardened Australians. He would have been a real asset at Wollongong, our Hugues, in trying to end the sequence of four losses.

When you got to Wollongong, you could see why the most powerful state in the country had been called New South Wales. Smoking chimneys punctuated the sky-line of this important coal-mining and steel centre fewer than 100 kilometres south of Sydney. It was a bit like the Swansea of the Pacific, and since there's no reason for NSW miners to have skulls any less solid than their Gallic cousins, it was never going to be a tea party.

New South Wales Central had a powerful pack of forwards and bossed the exchanges. Losing out in the head-to-heads, France tried in vain to open the game up but despite their superior speed and spontaneity, were simply snuffed out. A try from Voron and three Duplé goals were not enough to pull back a 12-4 half-time deficit and they slid to a 16-9 defeat. With six days to go to the first test, you could hardly call it encouraging. It was serious. The attack had plenty of quality and, at the same time, the pack had all the necessary power, speed and technique, but there had been too many youngsters thrown in too early. There was a marked absence of that cohesion essential to cope with huge rampaging Australians.

78

After thinking hard and long, Antoine Blain, Jean Duhau and René Duffort picked Berthomieu in the front row despite his injured hand. Hugues had gone to see Duhau the night before the match.

"I know you want me to have a rest, Jean, but you need an old head like me in that pack. If I'm not there to advise and encourage, they'll go to pieces. With plenty of strapping and a jab of novocaine, I can play."

Berthomieu played and he was superb. A ground record of 98,000 (700 more than in 1951, but I don't know how) packed the Cricket Ground, but the pitch was a sea of mud, right up the Kangaroos' street, with their stolid, direct style which avoided errors – and flair. France had lined up as follows:

Benausse; Ducasse, Merquey (captain), Rey, Voron; Jiminez, Dop; Vanel, Moulis, Berthomieu, Pambrun, Delaye, Duplé.

Australia had selected:

Churchill; Flannery, Wells, Watson, Kite; Henry, Holman; Bull, Kearney, Hall, Davies, Holloway, Diversi.

Merquey, Dop and Delaye were the only survivors from the 1951 tour, whereas Australia could call on eight who had played in that series or toured France in 1951-52. Full-back Churchill, the right-wing partnership of Flannery and Wells, and scrum-half Holman were picked in the backs, while the selectors went for four forwards who must rank among Australia's best-ever: Hall, Kearney and Bull to add steel to the front row, and Brian Davies to lend support in the second row.

All the French fears were realised. On a heavy pitch, the pack was slowly but mercilessly taken apart. Yet again, the French attacking machine was forced to concentrate on last-ditch defence.

There's little else to say about the game. With overwhelming territorial superiority, the Australians were never in danger. A brave display restricted them to a 5-0 half-time lead, through a Kite try converted by Davies. Holman's goal after the break stretched it to 7-0, but the Tricolors created a minor sensation a few minutes later by cutting the deficit to 7-5 with a Ducasse try converted by Duplé. The French threat, however, soon fizzled out, for while Benausse was off the field for treatment, the Kangaroos scored three tries in 10 minutes, one to huge centre Wells and two to quicksilver scrum-half, Keith Holman. With Davies adding two conversions, it was now 20-5. France eventually found some cohesion in the last 15 minutes and, though clearly in control, could only register a single try, by the courageous Berthomieu, to make the final score 20-8. After six defeats on the trot, the small group flew out next day to Queensland, not a happy hunting ground for France. Their faces weren't exactly glowing with confidence.

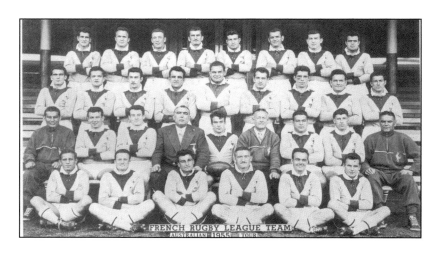

The 1955 French tourists:
From left: Back: R. Guilhem, A. Carrère, A. Delpoux, A. Savonne, M. Voron,
G. Berthomieu, F. Montrucolis, G. Benausse; Third row: F. Cantoni,
A. Save, C. Duple, J. Fabre, G. Delaye, J. Pambrun, J. Jammes, J. Vanel,
R. Rey; Second row: R. Duffort (coach), R. Moulis, F. Levy, A. Blain
(manager), J. Merquey (captain), B. Moore (masseur), J. Audoubert,
A. Jimenez, J. Duhau (coach); front: J. Dop, A. Ducasse, V. Larroudé,
R. Contrastin, S. Menichelli, C. Teisseire.

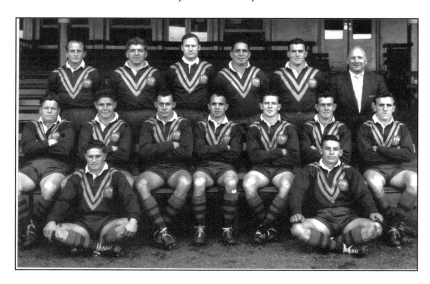

The Australia team for the 1955 third test against France:
Back: H. Crocker, H. Holloway, D. Flannery, D. Hall, B. Davies, V. Hey
(coach); seated: K. Kearney, D. Furner (reserve), A. Watson, C. Churchill
(captain), K. Holman, R. Kite, R. Poole; front: D. Henry (reserve), G. Laird;
absent: R. Bull. (Photo: Melba Studios, Sydney)

Martial Law

Antoine Blain, Jean Duhau and René Duffort were even more worried than the players as they left for Queensland, hardly the luckiest of venues for the 1951 team.

After reaching the state capital, the Tricolors lined up in a night match against a Brisbane Select that included internationals Hall, Davies and Watson. France had lost Voron and Berthomieu, both injured in the first test, as well as Delaye, left behind in a Sydney hospital with a fractured vertebra, but had got Contrastin back. His return was decisive and with him in full cry scoring twice, he inspired the Tricolors to produce an authentic 'Flying Frenchmen' performance. Fernand Cantoni, Delpoux and Save all got on the scoresheet and France left the Exhibition Ground 21-11 winners, with applause ringing in their ears.

At long last songs, smiles and jokes resurfaced in the changing-room. Here was real proof that France could come up with big games if they put in enthusiastic team performances. From now on, their efforts mustn't go to waste and they had to concentrate on the next objective, the important game against Queensland in Brisbane the following Saturday, 18 June. So that they could prepare better for this vital match, the triumvirate decided to sacrifice the tricky fixture against Toowoomba on the Wednesday.

While the first choice team stayed in Brisbane to train for the Queensland clash, the reserves, including Contrastin, who was in need of some game time, took a real hammering, 35-6. There were references in the papers to Waterloo, but the French camp was more worried by injuries to Contrastin, who suffered another pulled muscle, and Guilhem, with a knee strain picked up in the Toowoomba mud, than the big score.

Everyone was determined to put in a big performance against Queensland to gain the vital psychological edge. Bill Corbett, an habitual follower of international tours, wrote in the *Brisbane Telegraph:* "Discipline in this French camp is draconian. I've never known a team put up with such a strict regime." Antoine Blain still hadn't come to terms with the six straight defeats in New South Wales. The Turk knew that the future of the tour may well depend on the outcome of this Queensland game, and had declared martial law. Every fit man was put on a war footing from morning till night: training sessions, relaxing walks along the Brisbane River, meetings to discuss tactics and a curfew from 10pm. So the injured could feel as though they were contributing something to the general mobilisation, they limped and hobbled behind Antoine Blain to the thousand and one receptions put on for the tourists. Lord knows how many tankards were emptied and speeches digested by Berthomieu, Voron, Contrastin, Guilhem and Teisseire.

In the Gabba dressing rooms, on Saturday 18 June, one was convinced that France were at last ready to fulfil their potential. Even though the pitch was really heavy, one could sense a steely determination among the forwards. The front row of Vanel, Audoubert and Montrucolis was, in fact, the strongest that France had been able to turn out so far. They were three tough lads who knew each other's game well after graduating from the Lyons academy of forward play, the best there was at that time.

All the same, Queensland again started remarkably well and didn't let the Tricolors settle into their game plan. They threw everything at them from the start and scored almost immediately when France sloppily allowed the ball to bobble over the line from a scrum near their posts, and second-row Drew pounced. Full-back Pope improved the try and Queensland led 5-0, a setback which seemed to unsettle the visitors. Powerful winger Ryan went on a 50-yard break and, although Dop got in a last-ditch tackle, the Queenslanders were by now breathing fire and France were struggling. After a play-the-ball, second-row Furner slipped out a pass for centre Laird to cross and Pope to convert. Racing to a 10-0 lead after only a quarter of an hour, Queensland seemed irresistible.

After their second try, Queensland felt the need for a breather, which was the signal for the French pack, led by Montrucolis, to regroup. Very soon there was a big difference. The Tricolor forwards played a simple, disciplined game and engaged in a gigantic battle. The Queenslanders only gave an inch at a time, but they gave. Fifty yards out, with the crowd lifting the roof off, Montrucolis launched himself from a play-the-ball, beat three tackles one after the other and pulled clear. Glancing to his left, he saw the slim figure of Roger Rey, who took his pass on the 25 and streaked with those long thoroughbred strides under the posts. Gilbert Benausse's conversion narrowed the gap to 10-5.

Now the Tricolors were firing on all cylinders and Queensland had not a moment's respite. Montrucolis's pack bottled up their formidable opponents like they hadn't since the start of the tour, while behind them, the attacking trio of Benausse, Rey and Merquey oozed class. Queensland attacked but, like a coiled spring, Rey crash-tackled his opposing number, Laird, who dropped the ball. Merquey, ever alive to situations like that, gathered the ball at full speed, right under Watson's nose, to race between the posts. Benausse's easy conversion brought the scores back level at 10-10.

The forward battle raged, and it was clear that whichever pack yielded would lose the game. Unfortunately, the usually reliable

Dop came up with a crucial handling error. The ball had been lost in the mud, Australian scrum-half Connell booted it on and just as Dop went to gather he lost control as it rolled on the slippery surface. Connell was the first to react, tapped it over the line and touched down. With half an hour gone, Queensland had retaken the lead 15-10.

Covered in mud and drenched through the Tricolors might have been, but their spirits were not in the least dampened and they positively hurled themselves back into the fray. "Come on, Queensland!" howled the passionate terraces, but the home six were driven back by the French pack. Duplé launched an attack, Dop supported and the incomparable Gilbert Benausse plunged through a gap. With all avenues blocked, he kicked ahead and chased with those short, jerky strides. Outpacing everybody, he picked up on the bounce and dived over the line under half a dozen tacklers. Duplé failed to add the extras, but France had closed to 15-13 and, five minutes away from the break, they pulled out all the stops. French attacks came in continuous waves all over the pitch. Cantoni finally found a weak spot in the defensive wall and picked out Merquey who interpassed with him, then cheekily cut through. Rey was on hand to take the pass, chip full-back Pope, gather and dive over under the posts. Gilbert Benausse added the conversion and France led by three, 18-15, at half-time.

The big result which had eluded France since the tour began was within their grasp and they were in no mood to let it slip. But they still hadn't won this draining contest, which would leave them without an ounce of energy and the crowd without a voice. In fact, not long after the restart, full-back Pope landed a penalty which cut the deficit to 18-17.

The Queensland forwards shook their heads, pawed the ground and charged, launching themselves from deep, ball under arms and eyes looking nowhere but straight ahead. Their strategy was simple: let the tricky French see as little of the ball as possible and keep battering away until the defence had to give. To the crowd's obvious delight, they charged like wild bulls at the French line, and once again, the ground shook to, "Come on, Queensland! Come on, Queensland!" As Queensland increased the pressure, René Duffort and Jean Duhau looked anxiously at their watches. "They've had possession in our 25 for the last 15 minutes," commented Duffort.

Queensland may not have lost the ball but nor did the French lose their heads. Rather than build a wall, they spread a net to halt these frenetic attacks for it would have been suicide to take on the Queensland pack in head-to-head confrontation. More astutely, Vanel, Audoubert and Montrucolis decided to do it the Lyons way, rather reminiscent of the tactics Scipio Africanus used against

Hannibal's famous elephants at the Battle of Zama. The French pack realized they would risk breaking their necks if they tried a head-on approach, but noticed that their opponents just took it in with no intention of passing. What they did, then, was to let them drive it in, one at a time, so two Tricolors could wrap them up. Coming in at different angles, one tackled low while the other would go round the shoulders and topple the Queenslander – the 'pincer defence'.

A cruel 20 minutes ensued, then the blitz ended for Queensland lost patience with the unprofitable one-out tactics and, looking for something different to break the stalemate, opened it up. It didn't pay them, for their open play resulted in Merquey flying in to snatch full-back Pope's intended pass to Laird. Interceptions have always been Merquey's speciality, and leaving Laird and Pope rooted to the spot, he sprinted clear to the posts. Benausse converted and France led 23-17. Queensland were now exhausted and France controlled the last quarter of an hour.

'Dazzling Merquey Sees France Home', was the headline in the *Brisbane Telegraph.* Without wishing to take anything away from Merquey, the main factor in this vital win was not so much an individual's brilliant display as a patient team effort, by every single player, which changed the face of the tour.

The psychological blow had been struck. Now the Tricolors were rid of the 'Kangaroos are unbeatable' complex that had wormed its way into their subconscious and that day they developed the same winning attitude as in the glory days of 1951. The day after their win over Queensland, the French team overcame Central Queensland in Rockhampton 40-24. They then flew off to Barcaldine in the interior, but the flight was appalling and, on landing, their legs felt like cotton-wool.

"Gentlemen," said Jean Duhau who was just as sick as the players, "the plane was late and the game kicks off in half an hour, so I suggest we have a bit of a feast in the changing rooms. I've got everything we need in the kit-bag."

"Superb, Jean!" called out Voron, one of the few who could talk, "you're a real father to us!"

Duhau carefully unpacked the jerseys.

"Where's our snack?" asked Voron. "Here you are." And Duhau handed everyone an orange as if it were a roast pigeon and added, without the hint of a smile, "Leave a bit for half-time, mind. Don't over-fill your stomachs." Fat chance! Most of the party had got over the air-sickness but hunger had brought on terrible stomach cramps, and vegetarianism didn't seem to provide the remedy for rugby players. "Gentlemen, I'm going to let you into a little secret. In 1924, I was beaten in the final of the Army Championship by a boxer, I can't remember his name, but I do know he went on to enjoy a successful career. And why did I lose? Because I ate too much. To build up my strength, I would stuff myself with chicken, ham and roasts. Well, the bout ended with me being laid out for the count by some skinny shrimp. Ah well, get stuck in and enjoy your grub."

Jean Duhau's Army Championship tale had put everyone in a good mood and the lads took the field with hearts as light as their stomachs. They had an outclassed Western Queensland for dinner as the hungry French ran in seven tries in a 29-14 feast.

After an evening meal of giant turkey, the Tricolors flew to Cairns in the extreme north of Australia. Cairns, midway between the Tropic of Capricorn and the Equator, was an ideal place in which to spend the winter and a magnet for visitors from Melbourne and the rest of southern Australia. Although it was the end of June and right in the middle of the Australian winter, here, on the shores of the Coral Sea, one could enjoy the sunshine as if it were summer in the Riviera.

They spent the day relaxing under palm trees on Green Island, one of the marvels of the Great Barrier Reef, and really weren't all that keen on leaving to play in Cairns on a dusty, bare pitch, under a leaden sky. They started rather gingerly against North Queensland but in the heat of the action (if you could call it that) they raised the tempo. Under severe provocation from the home team's crude, rough-house tactics, the Tricolors exploded. Rarely had they played so brilliantly, even in the glory days of 1951, and the unfortunate locals, looking as miserable as pioneers without a beer since morning, were overwhelmed. France ran in an impressive number of tries, 14 to be exact, with Cantoni and Delpoux both scoring hat-tricks, Rey and Deroude two each and the others going to Vanel, Carrère, Audoubert and Levy. Gilbert Benausse, Puig-Aubert's pupil at Carcassonne, quickly followed in his master's footsteps by amassing 24 points with 10 conversions, a penalty and a drop-goal.

With another win under their belts, the Tricolors set off for Brisbane, stopping off just long enough to wallop another Queensland Select 42-26, scoring eight tries with Gilbert Benausse contributing eight conversions and a penalty.

France's triumphant return created a sensation in Brisbane. Journalists scrambled to interview Gilbert Benausse, a kicking prodigy hailed as the new Puig-Aubert. After all, hadn't he landed 40 out of 46 attempts in the last six matches?

Their reception was, in fact, so enthusiastic that the triumvirate, Antoine Blain, Jean Duhau and René Duffort, had to again declare martial law. "If we don't protect them from their friends, they'll turn out to be enemies," was Blain's view.

The friends that Blain was really talking about were the girls, who posed by far the greatest danger to the French. With headquarters slap-bang in the middle of Brisbane, the Tricolors in their elegant outfits were a massive attraction. The more sanguine French can't understand one of Australia's strangest crazes – collecting autographs. From morning till night, they had to sign balls, books, cards and simple scraps of paper.

Most determined of all were the serried ranks of young Australian girls who besieged the hotel from first thing in the morning. Most of them just wanted an autograph as a souvenir, but the bolder (and just as good-looking) ones wanted a closer, more personal relationship with the 'Gallant Frenchmen', as the women's magazines called them. Some of the lads hadn't a clue how to resist the charms of the Queensland beauties. It's not for me to throw any light on these trysts, but I'd be lying if I said they were isolated cases.

To avoid any repetition, Antoine Blain, Jean Duhau and René Duffort decided that they would personally look after their players' moral welfare. The curfew was fixed for 8pm and any player caught in the corridor without a good excuse, such as a call of nature, was fined £2. The three officials were to keep watch in turns and, to judge from results, a good night's sleep did wonders for the warriors' moral and physical welfare.

86

Dop gets tiddly

The second test was going to break all Brisbane records. The Gabba, which had held 35,000 and produced receipts of £8,952 in 1951, had sold 45,745 tickets and poured £14,467 into the coffers of the ARL.

For this vital match, Australia had kept faith with their famous pack which had performed marvels in the previous test, with one exception: at loose-forward, the tough all-action Crocker replaced Diversi who was not considered forceful enough for a match like this. Their chosen props were the colossal Duncan Hall and the aptly named Roy Bull. Retaining his hooking role was Ken Kearney who had the thighs of a weightlifter and the chest of a wrestler. So he could feel more at ease in the on-field exchanges, he was careful to leave his dentures in a little box in the changing room – after all, it wouldn't stop him biting. With brick outhouse Brian Davies paired in the second row with a real giant in Holloway, the Kangaroo pack looked useful. The Australian selectors hoped this collection of monsters would enable their classy backs to launch some telling attacks. Chunky Keith Holman was at scrum-half while the young Queenslander, Laird, took over at stand-off from Henry. Their centres, Wells and McCaffery, were both built like oak wardrobes and in Clive Churchill they had the complete full-back. No wonder the bookies were only offering 6/4 against the Aussies.

While Australia had only called up three newcomers in Laird, Crocker and McCaffery, France made wholesale changes. Gilbert Benausse, who was a great stand-off, had looked very uncomfortable at full-back so Dop took over the last line of defence. He had passed himself fit to play despite a nasty cough – our 'enfant terrible' having managed to catch a chill at the Equator through drinking beer that was too cold. The threequarter line of Ducasse, Merquey, Rey and Voron was kept intact, but stand-off Jimenez was replaced by Benausse. Dop had moved to full-back so his place was taken by the diminutive Teisseire, known as 'The Rat' for his ability to scuttle through the tightest of defences. Duplé, a clever, steady player, remained at loose-forward but the most radical reshuffle came in the engine room. Without the mobile Guy Delaye, in hospital since the first test, the selectors went for experience in the second row with two hard cases who would stand their corner in any company, Berthomieu and Save. Vanel, Audoubert and Montrucolis would again provide the steel in the front row.

There was drama right from the beginning. In the very first minute, France lost the ball near their own posts and stand-off

Laird collected to swoop over. Churchill converted and Australia led 5-0. It was a cruel blow and the crowd were already convinced that there would be a repeat of the overwhelming first test triumph.

The hulks in green dominated for much of the opening 10 minutes and it was noticeable that, just as in Sydney, the new play-the-ball rule, with the defence only a metre back, favoured a forward game. As it demanded power and determination rather than skill and intelligence, the Australians were able to exert continuous pressure. That immaculate kicker, Gilbert Benausse, managed to reduce the deficit to 5-2 with a penalty goal in the 13th minute then, two minutes later, sensation! Our pocket scrum-half Teisseire, The Rat, tricked Crocker and Holman and broke, supported by centres Merquey and Rey. The latter took Tesseire's pass and rocketed through the remains of the defence to score under the posts. Benausse's easy conversion gave France a 7-5 lead which was increased two minutes later with a further penalty.

The battle which raged seemed to be between Australian power and French flair, especially the subtlety of Teisseire and Benausse at half-back, and Merquet and Rey in the centres. France knew they must get on top of these big Kangaroos who just kept on coming and battering their way to the posts. A scrum went down and the blond Crocker smashed through, beating off two would-be tacklers to score near the posts. With Churchill missing the conversion, France held a slender 9-8 advantage. Only 20 minutes had gone and the Australian pack had established an alarming dominance. The fiery Crocker backed up a Davies break and scorched down the middle, beating the whole French defence with astonishing ease to score close to the sticks. Churchill again failed to add the extras, so Australia led 11-9.

Stung, our forwards regrouped. The game evened out, but Australian territorial advantage ended in penalty goals to Davies and Holman while Benausse could only manage one in reply.

The half-time whistle came with Australia 15-11 up, not a catastrophic deficit, except France had seemed unable to match the huge Aussies head-to-head. They had been willing enough but the home pack had them in a vice-like grip. A second-half ordeal was on the cards. Only one person in the dressing room believed France could come back, an Australian known only by his Christian name of Jules. He was a highly strung little old man who chattered constantly and never left the players' side all the time they were in Brisbane. In the 1914-18 War, he'd been with the Australian Expeditionary Force at the Battle of the Somme and returned to the forests of his native Queensland with the Croix de Guerre [a military medal] and a deep affection for everything French. Jules

Merquey arguing with the referee during the Sydney versus France match.
(Courtesy *Rugby League Journal*)

also spoke our language very well and was so delighted to see French people again that he would never stop cajoling: "Give these Australians a good hiding."

The players flopped exhausted on the benches. Dop shivered with a fever and Jules was beside himself: "Poor lads, poor lads. Cheer up; I'm convinced you're going to win." He put his arm round Dop's shoulders and told him, "Hang in there, Jeannot, this old man's brought you oranges from his own garden." "Listen, Jules," Dop wheezed in his ear, "that's no good to me. I'm coughing my guts up and I've got a raging fever. If you were a real friend, you'd fetch me a half-litre of warm red wine. Otherwise, I'll croak out there on the pitch." "You're crazy, Jeannot."

"Are you my friend?"

"Yes, of course I am!" And with that, Jules rushed out. His stay in France had made him more than usually resourceful, so he went up to the function room and commandeered a litre of Australian Burgundy. A quick sneak to the bar and he returned triumphantly, bumping everyone out of his way and clutching a tankard full of warm, sweetened red wine. Dop drained it in one gulp and followed his team-mates back out, legs a little unsteady and senses rather befuddled. In any other player, behaviour like this would have appeared peculiar, but Dop was a law unto himself and nobody down under bothered anymore.

The Australian avalanche continued after the interval. Laird and McCaffery set up an attack and winger Kite took the chance to skirt round the French defence for another try. Davies failed to convert, but soon landed a penalty for Australia to lead 20-11 after five minutes of the second half. Yet again, France tried to get back in it. A combined Teisseire-Benausse breakaway allowed Merquey to slice through the Australian defence and man-on-man with full-back Churchill, he beat him easily to score under the posts.

Again, the French threat didn't last long. Crocker - inevitably Crocker - broke through and stand-off Laird took his perfect pass at full speed to cross for the fifth Kangaroo try. Davies had no trouble converting. Worse followed soon afterwards as second-row Holloway crashed over for the sixth after a pile-driving run. With only 14 minutes left, Australia couldn't have been happier at 28-16.

As had often happened before when humiliation hung over them, the Tricolors hit back strongly. Vanel, Audoubert, Montrucolis, Berthomieu, Save and Duplé threw off the chains that had imprisoned them since the match kicked off. Several mighty hit-ups and the Kangaroo pack looked more drained than one would have expected, given their earlier superiority. There then followed the most breathtaking finale imaginable.

The crowd were astonished to realise their giants had used up a suicidal amount of energy. Bull, Kearney, Hall, Davies, Holloway and Crocker all of a sudden had lead in their boots, but France still had enough in the tank to mount an attack. 45,000 spectators looked at their watches. Twelve minutes to go and Australia were on the verge of winning the series, but now the French forwards were sweeping all over the pitch. They had nothing to lose, but time was not on their side.

That slippery will-o'-the-wisp, Jean Dop, counterattacked, sliced through the whole Australian team and with only Churchill to beat, fed Rey who went under the posts. Benausse converted to reduce the deficit to 28-21. Just seven points, but with only six minutes left, it seemed impossible. Everything France did posed a threat and drew cries of admiration, though the 'bobby-soxers' were squealing anxiously. Six, five, four, three minutes. The Australian time wasting was strangling France. Less than three minutes remained when Dop had another of his mad moments. Like an escaped lunatic, our 'Devil's Brother' swerved to the left, then to the right, took off towards the touchline, cut back into the middle, dummied, stopped, then hurtled off again. The decibel count rose as Dop swept right between the panic-stricken Australians like a rabbit shooting from its burrow. Thirty yards from the line, he served Merquey who, beating Churchill yet again, scored under the posts. Benausse converted and France trailed by only two points, 28-26.

The ground was going mad. "Come on, Frenchies! Come on, Frenchies!"

In the main stand, Antoine Blain was pale with emotion. Just for a second, he regretted this last-ditch stand. What good was there in fresh hope if you fell at the last fence? It was better to lose by a hatful than be pipped by two!

Drained of strength, the Kangaroos gritted their teeth and relied on running the clock down. Just over a minute left! In a desperate effort to free themselves from the French stranglehold that threatened to choke them of the last gasp of air, they put in a massive clearance kick.

Dop turned and collected the ball on his own line. The Kangaroos spread right across the pitch and chased him down. This was the final play, the last-chance saloon. Dop hesitated for a moment then launched himself. The racket was deafening with stands roaring and stamping feet. Dop feinted, then veered away from Davies's powerful grasp.

"Go on, little fellow!"

Still feeling the effects of the toddy, Dop disappeared right into the centre of those juggernauts. He jammed the brakes on, leaving a huge would-be tackler helpless in the dust and, at the very moment the hooter sounded, he passed to Ducasse. It was now or never. Ducasse sprinted all along the touchline and dived over in triumph by the corner flag. The most amazing comeback ever had left the ground stunned. France had won 29-28.

A tide of humanity invaded the pitch. Right in the middle of the throng, a little old man was waving his arms about like a madman, laughing and crying at the same time, and screaming in French with a delicious Australian accent: "It was Jules's plonk that did it. Jules's plonk."

The 1955 New Zealand versus France test matches

Jacques Fabre tries to tackle Bob Hawes in the first test
(Courtesy Robert Gate)

Jim Riddell with the ball in the second test, supported by George McDonald
and Cliff Johnson. (Courtesy Robert Gate)

Antoine Blain's prayer

Fresh confidence surged through the French party after their incredible win. Anything was possible provided they got down to some serious work and concentrated properly on the third and final test at the Sydney Cricket Ground, three weeks later on 23 July. They had one regret, that of losing Guy Delaye for the duration. He had come out of hospital, suffered a relapse at his first training session and taken the earliest flight to Paris. Not wishing to jeopardise their chances, the Tricolors turned down the bitter forward battles offered by every regional side. They won 46-17 at Gympie on 3 July, 19-10 at Ipswich on the 5th, but lost a close game 17-15 at Newcastle on the 9th. A hard-won 28-26 success against Sydney under-23s followed on 13 July, but then they went down 37-23 to New South Wales in Sydney on the 16th. Finally, on July 20, three days before the final test, they overcame Western Province 11-8 at Parkes.

For these less important fixtures, France were without their marvellous scrum-half Claude Teisseire with a knee injury, but had welcomed back renowned winger Contrastin. Avignon's Jacques Fabre had shown tremendous form and was drafted in at prop with Montrucolis joining Berthomieu in the second row. Duplé, who could fill in anywhere, took Teisseire's place at scrum-half and his vacant loose-forward berth went to Francis Levy, a Catalan with a Scot's red hair and a Welshman's love of mixing it. Finally, Contrastin came back in on the wing for Voron.

The Australians kept faith with the pack which had roughed up the French for more than an hour in Brisbane. They gave a vote of confidence to halves Holman and Laird, and to full-back Churchill, but made wholesale changes to the threequarter line which was thought to have allowed too much space to Dop, Merquey and Rey. Kite was retained on one wing, but with Wells and McCaffery dropped, Watson moved from the other wing to fill in at centre with Queensland young gun, Poole, taking the other spot and the great Denis Flannery coming in on the wing.

These, then, were the teams:
France: Dop; Contrastin, Merquey (captain), Rey, Ducasse, Benausse, Duplé, Fabre, Audoubert, Vanel, Montrucolis, Berthomieu; Levy.
Australia: Churchill (captain), Kite, Poole, Watson, Flannery, Laird, Holman; Bull, Kearney, Hall, Davies, Holloway; Crocker.

Despite the rain which had transformed the SCG into a quagmire, the ground was again jam-packed. On a pitch like this, the Australian game plan was basic: use the power of the pack to demolish the French defence. In the seventh minute, this strategy gained an early reward when several forward assaults on the

French line created a gap for second-row Davies to plunge over in the corner. Australia led 3-0 and Jean Duhau admitted that with the Australian pack so dominant, he feared a collapse.

But on this mud heap, the Kangaroos committed several blunders which halted their momentum and allowed France time to regroup. Now the pack had got back into the game, their offensive trio of Benausse, Merquey and Rey launched several stylish attacks. You felt that it needed just one good chance for France to get over, and it came in the 25th minute. Dop counterattacked, Merquey carried on the move and Rey, Duplé and Benausse combined to free Contrastin. This was just the opportunity Tintin had been waiting for and he marked his return to the side by steaming up the touchline to cross in the corner for the equalising try. Benausse failed to convert.

Passions rose on the pitch and the frenzied crowd bayed at the least hint of a score. Five minutes before the break, a huge roar greeted the Churchill penalty which restored Australia's lead at 5-3.

The Kangaroos wanted to exploit their advantage and cut loose after the resumption, trying to crash through the French pack with sheer power but, with Berthomieu setting a fine example, the Tricolors defended courageously. Even better, in the 54th minute, France exploded with incredibly quick handling considering the difficult conditions. Australia were forced to cover French attacks on both flanks until Merquey finally found a gap and fed Rey who sprinted through and handed on to Duplé. Jinking past winger Kite and Churchill, he saw Davies coming across to tackle him and turned the ball back inside for the supporting Ducasse to cross. Gilbert Benausse was having an off-day with his kicking, missed this second conversion and not long after, muffed a second penalty, but if he'd managed his usual 50 per cent success rate, France would by now have been 10-5 ahead. As it was, they led by an unconvincing 6-5.

Fifteen minutes from the end, the Australians were penalized but as Gilbert Benausse had failed with several attempts, he wasn't confident enough to take on a difficult kick from 42 yards wide out. Christian Duplé was the team's choice for this vital attempt for as well as being able to play centre, scrum-half and loose-forward, he was an excellent goalkicker. He concentrated, hit it perfectly and the ball sailed over the crossbar to ease France ahead 8-5.

The exhausted Australians had had to hold out for 14 minutes in Brisbane against a rampant France who snatched victory at the death. Now it was the Tricolors' turn to creak, drained by the relentless battle in the mud. A 12-point lead hadn't been enough for the Kangaroos, so could France survive with only three? It seemed unlikely, especially as Australia piled on relentless pressure.

Australian legend Clive Churchill
(Courtesy Robert Gate)

The whole team defended desperately, but tired as the Australians' furious attacks reached a crescendo. Three times the French pack dragged Aussies back from their in-goal before they could get the ball down. The crowd rose to both teams: the Kangaroos for forcing the French into last-ditch defence, and the Tricolors for their backs-to-the-wall resistance. With five minutes left, Antoine Blain couldn't bear the tension and quit the stand. In a complete daze, he stumbled down the spiral staircase into an empty dressing room. René Gluck, a French friend who lived in Sydney, was worried he was ill and followed him down. He found The Turk sitting there, alone, not watching the game through the big window, his noble head buried in his strong hands.

"What's up, Antoine?" "Nothing... I'm praying." And so he didn't see that fine referee, Jack Casey, penalise France for offside, close to the posts with a minute left. He guessed, from the deep silence which fell, that the Australians were playing their last, and most dangerous card, the up-and-under where the ball is booted high into the sky and seems to the defenders to hang forever as attackers steam after it en masse. Churchill put it up and they all chased, wreaking havoc in the French ranks. Oh, how badly they wanted that winning try. There was a wild scramble for the ball under the French posts, then a loud cry. Instinctively, Antoine Blain raised his head to see little Ducasse from Bordeaux, (called 'the bird that's fallen from the nest' by Jean Duhau, because he looked

95

just like a scrawny, docile child) turning strange somersaults in the middle of a scrimmage. Yes, shy Ducasse had caught it with eyes closed so he did not have to see them coming to get him, and had been saved by the final hooter. The win was not good news for the visitors from the Federation. Another four years of looking at the frightful silver wedding cake they called the Goodwill Trophy. France were still champions of the world.

The Tricolors said their goodbyes and left the technical gurus to their problems. These weren't minor because the Australian experts were even less inclined than in 1951 to believe that players of slight build, like Dop, Teisseire or Merquey, could play behind a less athletic pack and bamboozle the Kangaroos to defeat.

Before leaving for France, the Tricolors paid another visit to New Zealand, playing seven games in 19 days. They triumphed in the first test 19-9, but the Kiwis took the second 11-6 in a close match. This New Zealand section of the tour was, as always, simply an add-on designed solely to foster relations between the two federations. It rained so much during this trip to the land of the Maori that in Christchurch, the players paddled in a sea of mud beneath enormous cloudbursts. To avoid a second chill, Dop climbed up into the stand and players, referee and spectators were flabbergasted to see him come out disguised as a Newfoundlander in a huge ankle-length fisherman's coat and oilcloth cap. The journey home was quicker than in 1951: Auckland, Fiji, Hawaii, Los Angeles (where Jean Dop stopped off to see his American uncle), New York, and Paris. Even on an old-fashioned propeller-driven Super-Constellation, it barely took four days. At Le Bourget, the French party met up with friends, parents and several officials including Claude Devernois. Now that he'd conquered Australia, only the Himalayas were left.

IV. 1960: Incredible comeback

"Oh, the cheek of that nation!"
William III

France reached her peak and went downhill. It happens in all sports, and you must recognise the first signs of declining powers. Crowned champions of the world for a second time in 1955, they enjoyed one more season at the top and overcame New Zealand in a three-test home series, winning the first 24-7 in Toulouse, losing the second 31-22 in Lyons and taking the decider in Paris, 24-3. Then came the awful 1956-57 season when the Tricolors lost three tests in France against Australia, and the three-test series against Great Britain. Season 1957-58 wasn't brilliant either with Great Britain winning again.

Sportswriters are a strange breed who are always watching events which have never been played before and which will never be seen again. They catch the fleeting moment and pin it in their album of memories. So how could they fail to notice, that spring of 1959, the simultaneous revival of France with its 24-15 defeat of Great Britain, and the tragic end of that greatest of all Tricolors, Max Rousié, whose name is synonymous with rugby? Poor, dear Maxou, how you would have loved to have emerged from the gloom of your despair at the very moment your own beloved France moved back into the sunlight.

The aim of the French selectors was to come up with a team for summer 1960 in Australia which would be worthy of the name 'Tricolors'. So that they could make a better job of preparing for this third crusade down under, it was decided to sacrifice the 1959-60 international programme and view the Kangaroos' visit as a great opportunity to try out some new faces.

Admittedly, the selectors made the mistake of throwing in their union international signings, Barthe, Quaglio, Lacaze and Mantoulan, too quickly. But didn't the reshaped French team achieve a 20-18 victory over Great Britain in Toulouse, in an epic match that spring of 1960, and a 17-17 draw in the equally sensational return match in St Helens, which everyone expected them to lose? On the same warm evening as the famous Roanne versus Albi final, 8 May, France flew out of Toulouse for their third tour of the antipodes with only two survivors of the 1955 party: captain Antoine Jiminez and Gilbert Benausse. This, then, was how the party was made up:

Full-backs: Pierre Lacaze (Toulouse), Louis Poletti (Carcassonne).

Wingers: Jacques Dubon, Jean Foussat and Raymond Gruppi (Villeneuve), René Benausse (Lézignan), Jean Verges (Montpellier) and Alain Perducat (Roanne).
Centres: Gilbert Benausse (Lézignan), Claude Mantoulan (Roanne), Jean Darricau (Lyons).
Stand-offs: Antoine Jiminez (Villeneuve), Robert Moulinas (Avignon).
Scrum-halves: Bernard Fabre (Albi), Joseph Giraud (Montpellier).
Props: Aldo Quaglio (Roanne), Marcel Bescos (Albi), Angelo Boldini (Villeneuve), Francis Rossi (Marseilles).
Hookers: André Casas (XIII Catalan), André Vadon (Albi).
Second-rows: Jean Barthe and Robert Eramouspé (Roanne), Yves Mezard (Cavaillon), Roger Majoral (XIII Catalan).
Loose-forwards: André Lacaze (Villeneuve), Georges Fages (Albi), André Marty (Carcassonne).

Pen-Pictures of the 1960 tour party

1. Pierre Lacaze (Toulouse) Full-back. 10 stone 5 pounds; 5 feet 5 inches; 26; Commercial traveller. Former rugby union test full-back, 'Papillon' is a colourful successor to Puig-Aubert as an accurate goalkicker and drop-goal expert. An unorthodox, erratic, temperamental but superb attacking full-back.
2. Jean Verges (Montpellier) Winger. 11 stone 12 pounds; 5 feet 9 inches; 26; Bank clerk. A speedy winger or centre with a devastating sidestep that earned a try against Great Britain on his debut earlier this year.
3. Antoine Jiminez (Villeneuve) Captain. Centre. 11 stone 13 pounds; 5 feet 9 inches; 31; Schoolteacher. A versatile player who has won every honour with his club. Thrilled crowds in 1955 with wonderful positional play, speed and tactical awareness. Splendid footwork and mazy running create many openings. 'Totole' is a fine leader and complete gentleman.
4. Gilbert Benausse (Lézignan) Centre. 12 stone 2 pounds; 5 feet 9 inches; 28; Groundsman. 'Gigou' rates among the best-ever. France's most brilliant attacking force with tremendous pace over 30 or 40 yards. Made his first appearance for France as an 18 year-old, and has amassed 38 caps. Has an uncanny knack of knowing when to pass and tackle. Allies his brilliance to the team effort.
5. René Benausse (Lézignan) Winger. 12 stone 9 pounds; 5 feet 9 inches; 31; Accountant. Speedy elder brother of centre Gilbert. Represented France on the left wing against Great Britain in March 1960.
6. Claude Mantoulan (Roanne) Stand-off. 12 stone 2 pounds; 5 feet 7 inches; 24; Clerk. An outstanding talent, tipped as potentially France's best since the war. Rugby union international in 1959, he switched codes with great success, although some critics claim he kicks too much – a hang-over from his union days. A real star.
7. Bernard Fabre (Albi) Scrum-half. 11 stone 7 pounds; 5 feet 8 inches; 25; Municipal employee. Prone to injury, but absolutely brilliant when fit and on form. Enjoys terrific speed off the mark with elusive footwork.
8. Aldo Quaglio (Roanne) Prop. 15 stone 5 pounds; 5 feet 10 inches; 28; Textile worker. Tough, experienced rugby union test convert who made an

98

impressive international rugby league debut against Australia. Drives in straight and hard, and is a punishing scrummager. Has excellent defence.

9. André Casas (XIII Catalan) Hooker. 15 stone 5 pounds; 5 feet 7 inches; 26; Municipal employee. Test-hardened hooker who had the edge on Britain's brilliant Tommy Harris in the recent series. A crack utility player, capable of upsetting the tightest defence with his vigorous bursts.

10. Marcel Bescos (Albi) Prop. 15 stone 6 pounds; 5 feet 11 inches; 23; Fishmonger. One of the discoveries of the 1959-60 season. Former rugby union international with test experience against Australia. Robust, but adroit forward who handles well. An expert scrummager, but also very mobile.

11. Jean Barthe (Roanne) Second-row. 14 stone 7 pounds; 5 feet 11 inches; 28; Textile worker. 'Jean jean' had some difficulty adjusting after switching from union, where he starred in the wins in South Africa. Lost his league test place, but roared back with some barnstorming runs. He is now vice-captain and a vital cog in the French machine.

12. Robert Eramouspé (Roanne) Second-row. 13 stone 12 pounds; 5 feet 10 inches; 25; Pottery worker. 'Agnat' made his test debut versus Great Britain in 1958-59. Although he prefers running to tackling, his excellent positional sense and anticipation make him a constant threat.

13. André Lacaze (Villeneuve) Loose-forward. 13 stone 3 pounds; 5 feet 7 inches; 30; Adjuster. No relation to the full-back, Pierre. Another convert from rugby union, he has proved himself a fine cover defender and displays good ball-handling skills.

14. Louis Poletti (Carcassonne) Full-back. 10 stone 7 pounds; 5 feet 7 inches; 30; Locksmith. Another test player, he is very dependable on defence, but also a dangerous attacking force who links up well with his backs.

15. Raymond Gruppi (Villeneuve) Winger. 12 stone 5 pounds; 5 feet 10 inches; 23; Seedsman. Has also played test rugby league as a centre. A 200m sprint champion.

16. Jean Foussat (Villeneuve) Centre. 12 stone 5 pounds; 5 feet 8 inches; 29; Electrician. A star of the last World Cup, he was dropped but has regained his place on this tour. Fast, incisive runner who is equally at home on the wing or at stand-off.

17. Jean Darricau (Lyons) Centre. 12 stone 3 pounds; 5 feet 9 inches; 29; Industrial designer. Another player with real pace. Can prove his versatility on this, his first tour, by also playing as a winger or second-row.

18. Alain Perducat (Roanne) Centre. 11 stone 2 pounds; 5 feet 8 inches; 24; Commercial traveller. Joined the party as a last-minute replacement.

19. Robert Moulinas (Avignon) Stand-off. 11 stone 8 pounds; 5 feet 9 inches; 23; Male nurse. Stocky little player who made his test debut against Australia in December 1959. Has neat footwork and sound defence. Versatile.

20. Joseph Giraud (Montpellier) Scrum-half. 11 stone 1 pound; 5 feet 8 inches; 31; Wine producer. On his first tour, he shows great versatility. Skilful handler and courageous, he will not take a backward step.

21. Angelo Boldini (Villeneuve) Prop. 15 stone 7 pounds; 5 feet 11 inches; 31; Driver. Powerful packman with test experience who can mix it with the best. Punishing tackler and France's biggest forward.

22. André Vadon (Albi) Hooker. 12 stone 10 pounds; 5 feet 8 inches; 26; Farm worker. A specialist hooker on his first tour. Wins plenty of ball and is solid in the loose.

23. Francis Rossi (Marseilles) Prop. 13 stone 4 pounds; 5 feet 8 inches; 23; Importer. Fast, vigorous worker whose liveliness in the loose gives the tourists many options. Has not yet made his international debut.

24. Roger Majoral (XIII Catalan) Second-row. 14 stone 5 pounds; 5 feet 11 inches; 26; Farmer. Very fit forward on his first tour. Lively in the loose, and tackles with considerable impact.

25. Yves Mezard (Cavaillon) Second-row. 15 stone 5 pounds; 5 feet 11 inches; 28; Railway worker. One of the biggest in the party, he can also slot in at prop. Difficult to stop and a solid scrummager.

26. André Marty (Carcassonne) Loose-forward. 12 stone; 5 feet 8 inches; 30; Butcher. Dazzling player who is equally effective at the base of the scrum or at centre.

27. Georges Fages (Albi) Utility. 13 stone 2 pounds; 5 feet 8 inches; 26; Merchant. Former captain. Equally at home at hooker or half-back or loose-forward positions, so his value can not be overstated. A winner: brave and full of character, he organises brilliantly on the field.

28. Jacques Dubon (Villeneuve) Winger. 11 stone 2 pounds; 5 feet 6 inches; 29; Accountant. Tricky runner with fine turn of speed. Capable handler and dependable finisher.

Antoine Blain Manager. On his third tour down under, Antoine is known and respected everywhere the game is played. Converted successfully to rugby league after a distinguished international union career. Packing down at over 16 stones, he is a big man in every sense, managing to combine his role as secretary general with journalism at the *Midi Libre* in Montpellier.

Guy Vassall Assistant Manager. On his first tour, but he provides much-needed help to the manager, now that these visits are so demanding. An experienced administrator.

Jean Duhau Coach. Dual international forward who went on Galia's missionary tour in 1934. Has long experience of coaching and is on his third tour down under. Enjoyed plenty of success at club (Bordeaux) level and with the national team. An ever-present whose playing career was cut short by the war.

René Duffort Coach. Toured as a player in 1951 and here for the second time as coach. Known as 'The Craftsman' during his distinguished playing career with the famous Lyons club, he now manages to impart his know-how to every new generation of young players. Brilliant tactician and motivator.

Alain Perducat, hero of the recent Championship final and a last-minute selection, left a week later to join the others in Sydney. In effect, the Tricolors split into two teams in Jakarta, with the group led by Guy Vassal and René Duffort going on to Perth to play against Western Australia, while the rest, with Antoine Blain and Jean Duhau in charge, stopped off in Darwin for Northern

The 1960 French touring party.
Back: R. Benausse, A. Casas, G. Fages, A. Marty, W. Moore (trainer),
A. Foussat, F. Rossi, C. Mantoulan, A. Quaglio; standing: J. Verges,
R. Gruppi, A. Boldini, R. Majoral, M. Bescos, Y. Mezard, A. Lacaze,
R. Eramouspé, J. Darricau, J. Giraud; seated: J. Duhau (coach), A. Vadon,
J. Barthe, G. Vassal (assistant manager), A. Jiminez (captain), A. Blain
(manager), G. Benausse, B. Fabre, R. Duffort (coach); front: L. Poletti,
R. Moulinas, P. Lacaze, J. Dubon.

Territory's centenary celebrations. France marked their arrival in Australia with two victories: 42-14 in Darwin and 29-8 in Perth with the group which was to serve as the basis of the test team. In Perth, Gilbert Benausse and Mantoulan, creator of three tries, reigned supreme. 'Papillon' Lacaze put on a dazzling display, landing five conversions out of five and two penalties, one of which was a drop from 50 yards out, wide on the touchline.

It was a cheerful French party that booked into their usual headquarters at the Olympic Hotel with its cool triple rooms. Nothing had changed much: waitresses still thought they were doing you a favour when they condescended to bring your soup; the smoky pub was still crowded with drinkers and reeked of beer; the same, though somewhat faded, singer sat at the familiar out-of-tune piano, murdering the same old songs. They hardly had time to unpack their cases before René Duffort called a training session. He didn't have the personnel to take on the Kangaroos with brute force, so decided to do it the French way: beat them with speed and unsettle them with superb physical condition.

The team concentrated mainly on sprint sessions in the neighbouring parks or practising ball skills on the pitch next to the Cricket Ground. Under this regime, even Boldini started to lose weight! While René Duffort was in charge of the technical side,

Jean Duhau took on the task of engendering the mood of cheerfulness without which no French rugby player can survive. After a few days, he had given everyone a nickname. Poletti, slight and with a fragile look about him, became 'Guinguille' (beanpole). The proud, secretive Jean Barthe was 'Ben Hur'. Fages, who struggled to get up in the mornings, was the 'Koala', the sweet little bear-like creature which only opens its eyes to eat eucalyptus leaves. Then we had 'Captain F.F.I.', as Giraud was called after being promoted captain of the reserves, just because he was the oldest. Fabre, a good-looking lad with a splendid moustache, was 'Le danseur mondain' (the male escort) and Mezard with his lovely Provençal twang became 'Mon Beau' (old love), an expression he was always using, much to our delight. We also had 'Baby' Moulinas because he looked like a demure child, 'Santé' (cheers) Quaglio and 'l'aveugle' (blind man) Vadon since he was the only one to wear glasses. Finally, Bescos was the 'Benedien' (man from planet Benedie). Duhau claimed that anyone so much like a caveman had to be some Neanderthal throwback, sent from outer space to study earthlings. Even I didn't escape, becoming 'French L'Equipe' (French team) simply because this was the shortened version of 'special representative of the French newspaper *L'Equipe*', which Bill Moore, France's permanent masseur, thought up when he introduced me to officials.

Last of all were those who already had suitable nicknames which Duhau didn't think worth changing: 'Totole' Jiminez, 'Le Mantoule' Mantoulan, Pierre 'Papillon' (butterfly) Lacaze, 'Agnat' Eramouspé, Gilbert 'Gijou' Benausse and Antoine 'The Turk' Blain.

We had wins against Monaro Division, 25-17, in Canberra on 18 May, then in Newcastle, an important industrial area 100km north of Sydney, against a tough local outfit, 14-10, on Saturday 21 May. After jumping to the rather hasty conclusion that no-one could beat them, the Tricolors learned the very next day, Sunday, that any chink in the armour of a French touring team will be exploited by regional teams playing the game of their lives.

Those who hadn't played the day before flew to Kempsey. The flight was simply appalling. The little DC3 seemed on its last legs, struggled to gain altitude and pitched so much the team spent the journey with their faces buried in paper bags. Landing looked like being a disaster. Boldini was standing when the plane hit an air pocket on descent and landed on one tyre which promptly burst. Stumbling down the steps, the 'Flying Frenchmen' had glazed eyes and legs like jelly.

They received a warm welcome at Kempsey airport where an impressive fleet of American cars was waiting to take them in procession, complete with police outriders, into a town in carnival mode. With its broad streets and wooden buildings, Kempsey

actually opened the scoring in the fourth minute with a superb penalty by Papillon Lacaze for offside against the prop, Beattie. Not long after, Barnes equalised with a kick from 27 yards after a play-the-ball offence by Fages. This intense, raw thriller of a test was developing into a sensational duel between the two full-backs. After 11 minutes, Beattie's obstruction allowed Lacaze to edge France ahead 4-2 with an angled penalty from 37 yards but, yet again, Barnes replied four minutes later with a tremendous effort from the touchline, 47 yards out. Excitement reached fever pitch in the stands after a scrum close to the line when Gasnier went through a massive gap, devouring the yards with his thoroughbred grace. A try seemed inevitable when a French jersey rocketed after Gasnier, pegging him back with every stride, and dragged him down near the posts. Our saviour was none other than Gilbert Benausse. The French response was stunning. Fabre went clear, breaking clean through from behind a scrum. Jiminez, Benausse and Mantoulan kept the attack going and the crowd were on their feet when Lumsden, tracking over from the opposite wing, brought 'la Mantoule' to earth only two metres from the line. It was tit-for-tat all through the half, an even tastier clash of titans because they were so perfectly matched. The 'Killers' couldn't launch their devastating attacks because every French forward strained to bottle them up, a stranglehold which allowed our backs to show they were just as classy as their illustrious opponents. In the 35th minute, Australia took the lead for the first time, 6-4, when Barnes punished a hooking offence by Casas with a magnificent 42 yard penalty.

France now needed a convincing response or the game might so easily slip away from them. When Muir was penalised for feeding two minutes from the break, Pierre Lacaze had a penalty chance 32 yards out half-way in from touch, but the ball unfortunately sailed past the left-hand post. Seconds from the final whistle, skipper Jiminez broke through the Australian defence in midfield and, just as he was about to be closed down, fed Foussat on the right. Our winger swerved inside his opposite number, Irvine, came up to full-back Barnes, drew him and slung a long inside pass to Mantoulan. He never got it. Rasmussen tackled him before the ball came near. Col Pearce, who had refereed the game superbly up till then, was too far away and didn't spot Rasmussen's foul. He didn't blow up. Pity, if he hadn't been fouled, Mantoulan would probably have scored under the sticks. The least France should have got was a penalty 20 yards out in front of the posts which Papillon would certainly have landed.

Instead of being deservedly on level terms, France conversely found themselves losing ground at the start of the second half. Barnes's fourth penalty, for feeding by Fabre, gave Australia an 8-4 lead in the 55th minute. Was the gap too big to close? Not at all. Col Pearce was very strict at scrums and three minutes after Fabre's penalty, it was Muir's turn to be pulled up. Lacaze landed the kick and cut the deficit to 8-6. Pandemonium reigned on the terraces. An Australian was so overwrought by the French domination that he dropped dead with a heart attack.

Nerves were on edge. France attacked relentlessly but Australia clung to the narrow two point advantage. A try, one little try, and France would win. Mantoulan intercepted, but was hauled down a few metres short. Gilbert Benausse broke and kicked ahead. Foussat popped up behind the Australian line with no-one near him, but the luck of the bounce went against him and a try went begging. And the hand of the clock ticked on. Five, four, three, two, one minute. In one last desperate assault, the French hurled themselves at the green wall. The Kangaroo defence was panicking and cracks were beginning to appear as the French, buoyed by the delirious crowd, launched one last frantic attack. Try under the posts. No, five metre scrum.

Last few seconds, final anguish, the clock already on zero, with Col Pearce still in complete control as these two giants clashed in one final confrontation. France had the ball and a winning try was possible as long as they kept the pressure on the exhausted Aussies who wanted that ball at any price, even at the expense of a penalty. Kelly slipped off his props and Mr Pearce blew for loose-arm just as the clock sounded the knell. The game would end with a Pierre Lacaze penalty attempt that his team-mates could hardly bear to watch. Papillon had never taken so much care over such an easy-looking kick. The whole ground fell silent. Then, an explosion of joy; the kick had succeeded and France had snatched an 8-8 draw in the most thrilling game ever seen at the SCG. The Sydney crowd had gone mental which summed up how delighted Australians were to see the Tricolors again, their Prince Charmings of rugby, and how happy they were to have seen justice done.

Few survivors

There was hardly time to break open the Champagne before France had to leave for Queensland, where they made a sensational start in a night match, against Brisbane, on Monday 13 June. The weather was beautifully mild, the turf at the Exhibition Ground perfect and the Tricolors, after a lacklustre first half, got the upper hand as their backs began to punch holes in the home defence. That's when the local referee, a Mr Purtell, began to rain more penalties down on France than Mr Punch suffers blows on his head. The Tricolors didn't like it one little bit. There was much palaver and it was even claimed that a touch judge had come in to support his superior's decision and had received, in the Brisbane night, a sly kick up the backside. It was said to have been the toe-end of Gilbert Benausse's boot, but a lot of things are said at night, in Brisbane.

These incidents boosted France's popularity considerably, for it was felt in Brisbane that the 'fiery Frenchmen' had been well and truly stitched up. The feminine press led the campaign for the Tricolors and this article appeared on the women's page in the *Telegraph*: "The Tricolors are especially attractive with their lovely dark eyes, well-groomed hair, perfect nails and elegant outfits. These players, who are considered to be extremely rugged on the pitch, show such refinement in their everyday lives that they make themselves even more fanciable by using special scented lotions after a shave or a shower."

Saturday 18 June, must go down as a black day in the French calendar. With Barthe rested, they went down 30-18 to Queensland whose famous pack, the 'Killers', were still smarting from their humiliation in last Saturday's test. Even more serious, this defeat was in great part due to an injury to Gilbert Benausse, which deprived France of her star player, and chief attacking force, for the rest of the tour. Luckily, with the exception of Barthe, who had to have fluid drawn off his knee, and Darricau, who went down with tonsillitis, all the others recovered.

On the day after the Queensland defeat, Joseph Giraud captained a team of 13 different players to a 33-10 win over Wide Bay in Maryborough, north of Brisbane. They drew a lot of encouragement from this game: Quaglio made a successful reappearance, while new elements like Boldini, Vadon, André Lacaze, Mezard, Poletti, Perducat, Dubon and Giraud all pitched in together to make the changes work. I've already said many times before how touched we were by the genuine friendship the Australians extended to the French. The Maryborough officials bent over backwards to satisfy our every wish and one of them even came one night to find Jean Duhau and confided: "You know we've got some marvellous snakes round here. You can find some superb specimens in the local sugar cane plantations: blacks, greens, striped ones. If you want a few dozen before the second test, just let me know."

Now don't go thinking that Jean Duhau harboured ambitions of becoming a fakir. He just fancied a leg-pull. The Australian journalists were very keen on minor details of the players' private lives and how they prepared for matches. Before the first test, Jim Mathers had asked Jean Duhau if the French took any tonics to pep them up on the pitch. "Certainly," he replied. "The night before a Test, I give my lads snakes."

"Huh, you're all peculiar, you French! You already eat frogs' legs and snails and now you sit down to eat boas!"

"Oh no, not big snakes, just little vipers only as thick as your thumb. You remove the head, because of the venom, boil them up and then put them in jars. Vipers give you unbelievable energy."

"Good grief! Vipers..." Jim Mathers left shaking his head, but after the astonishing first test result, he penned a sensational article in the *Daily Mirror,* entitled "The French Secret", and ended his piece as follows: "The trouble with our French friends is that they'll run out of snakes before the end of the tour."

That nice Maryborough official read this cry for help and offered to send the French team fresh supplies. Jean Duhau went along with it. "Thank you so much, you really are too kind, but the French Federation has just sent us a crate by air mail." The visitor took his leave, content that France had wanted for nothing in his fine town.

France enjoyed a run of victories in Queensland. First came the 13-8 win over Central Queensland in a night match at Rockhampton. Despite a tropical storm transforming the pitch into a bog, France won in grand style. Boldini, Mezard, Vadon, Perducat, Mantoulan, Gruppi and Foussat were the pick of the bunch, but especially Quaglio, who played like a demon. What worried them was Papillon Lacaze's puzzling lack of success with the boot, for he missed four easy kicks.

The weekend of 25-26 June gave the selectors the chance to run the rule over their available options. With Barthe returning, it left 25 fit and three injured: Gilbert Benausse out for the rest of the tour, René Benausse with a pulled thigh muscle from Maryborough, and Moulinas with a knee problem, again sustained in Maryborough. André Lacaze, who played wing in Cairns and loose-forward in Townsville, was the only one picked for both matches.

At Cairns, on the Saturday, under a tropical sun and in a blinding dust storm, the Tricolors won easily enough, 26-15 against Far North Queensland, but you couldn't call it a team effort.

In Townsville the following morning, the players went to see the Australian Olympic swimming squad train. For fully three hours, they observed the extraordinary routines that world stars like the Konrads, Devitt, Rose, Henricks and Dawn Fraser went through. In the afternoon, the swimmers returned the compliment and were keen spectators as France beat North Queensland 22-5. Fabre was man-of-the-match, outstanding in attack and defence. On the other hand, everyone was more and more worried about what had happened to Pierre Lacaze's magic boot, after he missed another four relatively easy kicks.

With four wins in four matches, France returned to Brisbane with heads held high. While the reserves settled into their Australian Hotel headquarters in the city centre, the 16-man test squad took themselves off to the Regatta Hotel, on the quiet banks of the Brisbane River, a delightful half-board establishment smothered with tropical vegetation. Life there was peaceful, but as well as concentrating on a second test which was on everyone's lips, the Tricolors could examine the reasoning behind the Kangaroo selectors' wholesale changes. In effect, Australia had changed tack. The famous Queensland forwards, the 'Killers', had been nullified in Sydney and they had to find a new way of winning, so organised two back-to-back matches between Queensland and New South Wales while France were up in the north. In the first game, the Queensland pack still bossed proceedings, but in the next, NSW were streets ahead. And so observing the law of the jungle, the Australian selectors ditched the Queenslanders, with the exception of Rasmussen, and brought back the old hands: centre Wells to team up again with Gasnier and forwards Mossop, Provan and Hambly.

Australia's line-up was enough to put anyone off with two 6 feet 3 inches props in Mossop and Rasmussen, and the huge 6 feet 4 inches Provan paired with 'Dynamite' Hambly in the second row. There were some shrewd selections in the strongest-ever Australian team with a huge pack of forwards the French called the 'Monsters', a stone and a half heavier and a head taller per man. Behind these incomparable forwards was a dazzling threequarter line in which Wells, with his 15 stones of muscle, combined with the brilliant, classy Gasnier. Finally, on the wing they had Lionel Morgan, the 'Black Arrow', Brisbane's favourite son and the first Aboriginal international.

France had gone for cohesion and picked the whole Villeneuve threequarter line: Dubon, Jiminez, Foussat and Gruppi. Albi provided the loose-forward-scrum-half link in Fages and Fabre, while the scrum-half and hooker partnership consisted of Fabre and Vadon. Barthe and Eramouspé formed a Roanne second row.

These, then, were the teams on Saturday 2 July:

Australia. Barnes (captain), Irvine, Wells, Gasnier, Morgan, Banks, Bugden, Mossop, Rayner, Rasmussen, Provan, Hambly, Raper.

France. P. Lacaze, Dubon, Jiminez (captain), Foussat, Gruppi; Mantoulan, Fabre, Bescos, Vadon, Quaglio, Barthe, Eramouspé, Fages.

You've got to remember that this French team didn't exactly fill us with confidence. The forwards, especially Bescos and Fages, were showing signs of weariness, but the Australian team was magnificent, apparently without weaknesses. "Disaster or sensational victory in the second test in Brisbane tomorrow?" ran the headline in the pessimistic article I sent to *L'Equipe* the night before the match, and I finished: "We're terrified that the French forwards will repeat their mistakes of not tackling low and falling into the trap of taking on the Kangaroos in a physical battle. If they do, the defence will soon disintegrate and we will be looking at another disaster like the one we suffered only recently."

Inky black clouds rolled round a threatening Brisbane sky, but despite the storm brewing, the Exhibition Ground had filled nicely. The crowd had encroached a fair way over onto the grass and the pitch itself was only just clear. At first sight, France didn't have the look of winners. The pack gave the 'monsters' too much freedom and soon they were living up to their name with France needing every last drop of energy to keep them out.

Alas, catastrophe loomed after some terrible bad luck. The first blow came right at the beginning when Fabre, France's key player, suffered a knee injury in the second minute and hobbled through the rest of the game. After seven minutes, Foussat was knocked unconscious by the giant Provan's knee and he had to leave the pitch. Nevertheless, the French backs put on a few moves which were only just foiled and, at half-time, the Aussies were not out of sight at 18-4.

Just after the restart, it was Fages' turn to go down with a knee injury and he, too, finished the game limping badly. Foussat had come back on, but fell awkwardly under the enormous Provan and retired for good with a dislocated collarbone which ruled him out of the rest of the tour. You can't win a game of rugby league with only 10 fit players, for there's no safety net to save you and France collapsed to a 56-6 hiding. It was hard to bear, much too hard.

Feeling as though they were on the retreat from Moscow, they dug deep, and calling on the few fit players available, outclassed Ipswich 33-19 on 6 July. Boldini, Poletti, Giraud, Marty, Mezard, Verges and André Lacaze had tremendous games, but unfortunately, Majoral picked up a groin strain, Mezard a rib injury and Boldini was unlucky enough to sustain a horrendous gash to his tongue from an Australian head. Without a word of a lie, if the blow had been any worse, a piece of his tongue would have fallen onto the Ipswich turf. Poor Angelo, the guy everyone liked for his plumpness, impressive power and his obsession for arguing with referees. The press had christened him 'The Bold Boldini', but he was reduced to silence and a diet of milk and macaroni.

In Toowoomba, France met the best team in Queensland and showed admirable guts and determination in the face of adversity. But who rattled Pierre Lacaze's cage that day? We knew that our Papillon had mysteriously misplaced his famous kicking boots. In Toowoomba, he had again missed two relatively easy kicks and when the next chance came, René Duffort on the touchline ordered him to hand over to his namesake, André Lacaze. Papillon started grumbling and throwing his arms about much to the amusement of the near 20,000 crowd. And then, trying to prove how clever he was, he indulged in some acrobatics which resulted in a try under the posts to the opposition winger, Lohman. This provoked not just hoots of laughter in the crowd, but real fury in Guy Vassal, René Duffort and the Tricolors.

To this gift of five points, you can add a further handicap: injuries to Gruppi with his knee and André Lacaze with a pulled rib muscle. All the same, France snatched a heroic 21-21 draw, but with only a week to go before the third test, three more players had been ruled out: André Lacaze and Gruppi injured and Pierre Lacaze suspended as a disciplinary measure.

Next morning, the Tricolors left again for New South Wales where their last-but-one game was scheduled for Armidale, 1,100 metres up in the harsh Blue Mountain air. On their retreat from Queensland, France registered another pyrrhic victory. In a freezing drizzle, they got the better of Northern Districts 24-10, but their bad luck continued and the situation became desperate. First Verges pulled a muscle in his chest and had to drop back to full-back instead of Poletti, but could hardly move and caught a chill. Marty moved onto the wing but fell awkwardly and injured his shoulder.

To complete this tale of woe, the very last second saw Perducat, with not a soul near him, dislocate his collarbone scoring the final try. The morning after, they flew off in the rain to Sydney. The little DC3 was so loaded-up it couldn't accommodate Quaglio's big suitcase and drawing on its last reserves of power, struggled to haul itself up into the air in the last few metres, from the waterlogged mud runway. Poor, crippled France in a nutshell.

Auckland 1960: Marcel Bescos is sent off in the first test.
The mud he threw at the referee is ringed.
(Photo courtesy Louis Bonnery)

Programmes from the 1960 tour:

Left: The third test against Australia.

Right: The second test against New Zealand.

Walking dead

On their arrival back in Sydney, the French party looked very much like an army in retreat. Relentless rain flooded the city as they rested in their base, nursing their wounds. Bill Moore dashed from room to room, massaging one, treating another. No more visitors called at the Olympic Hotel for no one is interested in you when you're down.

The press warned the Australian selectors: "Be careful. Don't count on an easy win over France. Don't take victory for granted even if they're on their last legs."

The Tricolors made a pitiful sight. Antoine Blain met Guy Vassal, Jean Duhau and René Duffort in his room to go over the injury list: Gilbert Benausse knee, René Benausse pulled thigh muscle, Gruppi knee, Foussat shoulder, Perducat shoulder, Verges pulled muscle and tonsillitis, Moulinas knee, Fages knee, Marty shoulder, André Lacaze pulled muscle, Mezard ribs, Boldini tongue, Rossi head, Majoral pulled groin muscle, Darricau dead leg and, finally, 'Papillon' Lacaze disciplined. That made 16 out of 28 unavailable with only these 12 more-or-less fit for action: Poletti, Dubon, Mantoulan, Fabre, Jiminez, Giraud, Barthe, Eramouspé, Quaglio, Bescos, Vadon and Casas - and these last two were both specialist hookers.

Two of the less seriously injured would therefore have to play. Boldini's gashed tongue hadn't yet healed, but he could run and signified his readiness to play – with sign language. Marty was called up for the second vacancy. His shoulder was still giving him trouble but, with a piece of thick foam, the sort you stuff armchairs with, he could do a job for us on the wing. Australia let it be known that there would be only one change in their super-team from the second test, which in fact would strengthen it, with fiery young Boden replacing the old fox, Banks.

Antoine Blain said nothing until 14 July and the famous visit to Botany Bay when France regrouped and took fresh heart from the simple sight of a faded tricolour jersey, whose rips and tears told of many a past battle. That was the day he chose to announce to Australia at large the most incredible team:

Poletti, Dubon, Mantoulan, Fabre, Marty, Jiminez (captain), Giraud, Bescos, Vadon, Boldini, Quaglio, Eramouspé, Barthe.

All the Australian sporting press were in the room: Bill Corbett, Tom Goodman, George Crawford, Jack Reardon, Alan Clarson, Ernie Christiensen. They looked at him dumbfounded. "How," they thought, "can you play a prop like Quaglio in the second row; a second-row, Barthe, at loose-forward; loose-forward Marty on the wing; scrum-half Fabre in the centre? These Frenchies must be really badly off. Tomorrow, Sydney Cricket Ground's going to witness the biggest hammering Australia's ever dished out."

They made their way out slowly, sad smiles on their faces and speaking in low voices as if leaving a house of sorrow. We were left alone except for good old Philippe who was muttering in the corridor, tears in his eyes: "What bad luck! What bad luck! I'm going to stick my knife in the ground…"

Poor old Philippe was going to call on the heavens to help France. But did we want sun? Wouldn't a deluge be better to slow down the executioners? Philippe's knife brought sun. The crowd assembled as usual, but this time more curious than passionate. Bookies weren't taking bets on the outcome, just how many Australia would win by. Business was brisk. In the dressing room, the French changed slowly. Jean Duhau handed out the jerseys and tried to lighten the atmosphere. "Now then, Barthe, someone once told me you were the best union forward in the world. I'm not saying he was wrong, but up till now, all you've shown in league are glimpses. Right, show us what you can do this afternoon. And you, Boldini, you're the only one who's managed to put weight on during the tour. I know you've got a split tongue, but in your case that's an advantage since you won't waste time arguing with the referee. Oh yes, and Angelo, you have a marvellous habit of going to sleep in the 25 so do try and take your nap in theirs, not ours. Hey, 'Guinguille' (Poletti)! If you carry on sidestepping for no reason, you'll end up with legs like knotted string…"

He had a word for everyone and soon smiles came back on faces. At last, they were ready and that's when Antoine Blain made his entrance. The Turk looked drawn and his face was pale. This tour had ruined the old warrior's health and he was troubled with his heart. The players knew this and that's why his words had such an effect on them.

"Gentlemen, in the two months we've been together, you will have realised that I'm not your supervisor, not a policeman nor a warder, but your friend. Friends must speak frankly. You all know I'm knackered, so I'll ask you, the last of many French teams I have loved, for one final big favour. A French win." Antoine Blain couldn't speak any more. For the first time, tears rolled down his lined cheeks.

People had come to bury them, but they had been reborn. France drew on supernatural resources they never knew they had and hurled themselves into battle with a passion. This had seemed to be no more than a last stand, a swansong and the crowd in Sydney, who had always had a soft spot for the 'Flying Frenchmen', had come along just to applaud their gallant show of courage. France started off like a whirlwind, but to those watching, this was just a superb act of folly, but folly all the same. By burning up all

116

The Australia team for the 1960 third test against France: Back:
R. Budgen, K. Irvine, C. Churchill (coach), F. Drake (reserve), W. Rayner;
first row: R. Boden, H. Wells, E. Rasmussen, L. Morgan, G. Parcell
(reserve), J. Raper; seated: R. Gasnier, N. Provan, K. Barnes (captain),
R. Mossop, B. Hambly. (Photo: Melba Studio, Sydney)

their energy like that, the French were rushing to disaster. The
star-studded Australian team, so impressive and seemingly
unbeatable, appeared taken aback by such an opening. How could
a team so ravaged by misfortune come back like that? It was one
of rugby's mysteries and a wonderful example of putting country
before self.

The French forwards were forced to intensify their defensive
efforts as the Australians launched devastating raids. The huge
Provan seemed to want to break the blockade by himself, but was
cut down with crunching tackles by Barthe, Bescos, Boldini or
Quaglio. Rasmussen, Hambly, Rayner and Mossop all suffered the
same fate for our six forwards were like a dozen demons, thwarting
their opponents' designs before coming back themselves to smash
holes in the green Australian wall. Little by little, surprise changed
to admiration, for the French defence was so fierce the Kangaroos
could hardly make a yard. France conjured up three opportunities
to score but just couldn't force their way over at the last moment,
and had to wait until the 38th minute to take the lead through a
Mantoulan penalty. The Tricolors trudged off to the dressing-rooms
at half-time to a standing ovation, for the whole ground
appreciated how they had risen above their problems with such
panache.

On the resumption, everyone thought it was only a matter of time before the formidable Australian machine would demolish French resistance but the crazy boldness continued. Even better, our threequarters started to hurl themselves into all-out attack on the back of the suicidal efforts of their forwards. Three times Marty found himself in the clear and a winger, or a fit Marty, would have gone between the posts for a hat-trick, but with his unfortunate shoulder injury he found it difficult to run normally and was overhauled a yard short. To preserve the narrow 2-0 lead, the 'Monsters' had to be driven back to their lair.

The whole stadium held its breath as neither side could get on top. A temple of rugby fell silent. I admired the wholehearted effort the Tricolors were putting in but feared they would collapse, for their line was tested more and more while the narrow safety margin stayed the same.

Sitting alongside me, injured team-mates chewed their fingernails. Finally, our fervent prayers were answered when Gasnier, the great Gasnier, lost the ball under a Bernard Fabre crash tackle. That little jack-in-the-box, Dubon, swooped and sprinted between the posts for a try which Mantoulan converted to give France a 7-0 lead.

Now it was danger time. The Kangaroos' pride was hurt and they roared into the attack with a fury that frequently went over the top. The atmosphere became very tense. The Australians failed to find a chink in our armour and had come to realise that the Brisbane result had been distorted by injuries. Yet they couldn't believe they were being outplayed by a French team they thought were on their knees only a fortnight before. The Australian colossus joined battle so furiously you feared that one last assault would overturn the Tricolors' hard-won advantage. Our pack was soaking up such fantastic pressure, you could sense their strength ebbing away.

If relentless Australian pressure couldn't break us down, could one stupid incident open the door? The atmosphere was, by now, stormy and in a desperate Australian attack, Irvine got away but was tackled in our 25 by Marty and Poletti and lay on the touchline, groggy. Fabre reacted quickly, aimed a huge kick at the loose ball and hoofed it in touch. But referee Lawler had spotted that Irvine hadn't got up and thinking that Fabre had caught him, ordered him off.

The French were staggered but, despite heated protests, nothing could change Mr Lawler's decision even though Irvine, who had only been stunned by the tackle, had resumed his position. To restore some semblance of order to the match, Blain and Duhau asked the unfortunate Fabre, now in tears, to leave the pitch. Now France were without a vital piece of the jigsaw, for with such an effective marker off the field, Wells cut through up the middle and fed 'Black Arrow' Morgan who put Bugden in for a try under the posts converted by Barnes.

The last three minutes were unbearable for, having closed the gap to 7-5, Australia attacked with savage power. France, shattered by the disaster at Brisbane and robbed of victory they deserved in the first test, were terrified they would be cheated of their hour of glory. Our pack, with their backs against the wall, were just magnificent. They had put so much pride and effort into this, their finest hour. Barthe charged in like a madman and, even with four Australians hanging off him, still managed to make ground. Boldini, Bescos, then Eramouspé came up in support as they surged majestically towards the Australian try-line, but Vadon just failed to cross.

At last, the bell rang and the crowd's roar saluted France's triumphant comeback. No dressing room has seemed so close, so fraternal as France's that day. Black and blue, the Tricolors collapsed on the benches. Faces streaked with mud, sweat and blood, they were dead with exhaustion but savoured the heady draught of victory. We stayed there a long time, a bunch of mates with minds blank but hearts full of joy. It was the kind of pleasure you can't buy, which no-one can understand unless he's played the game, a brotherhood, a religion that they call rugby.

Right after the game, they laid on a farewell banquet in the big room at the Sydney Cricket Ground. Everyone was there, Australian Board members and famous internationals who had contributed so much to the glory of the Kangaroos. There, too, was the present great Australian team, the finest and most powerful seen in the last 50 years. All that was missing was France. Finally, they appeared at the top of the staircase, a combination of heroes and cripples. As one, 100 all-time greats rose and, without saying a word, began to clap. The applause went on a long time, such a long time, until the last Tricolor took his place at the top table.

Appendix: Details of matches played in Australia and New Zealand in 1951, 1955 and 1960

1951: First French tour

Australia

23 May	W	France 37 Monaro Division 12 (Canberra)
26 May	W	France 12 Newcastle 8 (Newcastle)
30 May	W	France 26 Western Division 24 (Forbes)
2 June	D	France 19 Sydney 19 (Sydney)
6 June	L	France 10 Riverina 20 (Albury)
11 June	**W**	**France 26 Australia 15 (Sydney)**
13 June	W	France 29 Northern Division 12 (Armidale)
16 June	D	France 22 Queensland 22 (Brisbane)
20 June	W	France 38 Central Queensland 14 (Rockhampton)
23 June	W	France 50 North Queensland 17 (Townsville)
27 June	W	France 44 Wide Bay 19 (Bundaberg)
29 June	**L**	**France 11 Australia 23 (Brisbane)**
4 July	W	France 17 Brisbane 16 (Brisbane)
7 July	W	France 20 Toowoomba 17 (Toowoomba)
11 July	W	France 33 North Coast 9 (Lismore)
14 July	D	France 14 New South Wales 14 (Sydney)
15 July	W	France 24 Southern Division 13 (Wollongong)
21 July	**W**	**France 35 Australia 14 (Sydney)**
15 August	L	France 11 New South Wales XIII 29 (Sydney)
18 August	W	France 34 Australian XIII 17 (Melbourne)
24 August	W	France 70 Western Australia 23 (Perth)

Played 21, won 15, drawn 3, lost 3. Points: F 582, A: 357.

New Zealand

25 July	W	France 5 West Coast 2 (Greymouth)
28 July	W	France 13 Canterbury 7 (Christchurch)
30 July	W	France 26 Wellington 13 (Wellington)
4 August	**L**	**France 15 New Zealand 16 (Auckland)**
6 August	W	France 15 Auckland 10 (Auckland)
9 August	W	France 25 Auckland South 7 (Hamilton)
11 August	W	France 23 Taranaki 7 (New Plymouth)

Played 7, won 6, drawn 0, lost 1. Points: F: 122, A: 62.

Overall: Played 28, won 21, drawn 3, lost 4. Points: F: 704, A: 419.

1951 Australian match details

23 May France 37 Monaro Division 12
Manuka Oval, Canberra
Monaro Division: M. Preston (Queanbeyan), D. Stewart (Bombala), D. McRitchie (Queanbeyan), D. Hodges (Adaminaby), T. Fogarty (Goulburn), P. Schumack (Bega), K. Brogan (Cooma) (c), E. Schell (N. Canberra), K. Fogarty (Goulburn), K. Barber (Bega), B. Grant (Eden), R. Alexander (Canberra), P. Rankin (N. Canberra).
France: Puig-Aubert, Lespes, Comes, André, Contrastin, Caillou (c), Dop, Bartoletti, Genoud, Beraud, Lopez, Brousse, Calixte.
Referee: A. Nichols. Touch judges: L. Fenning & J. Arnold.
France: T: Lopez 2, Comes 2, Genoud, Contrastin, André; G: Puig-Aubert 7, Lopez.
Monaro: T: Stewart, Alexander; G: Preston 3.
Weather: good. Att. 5,000. (£880) KO 3pm.

120

26 May France 12 Newcastle 8

Newcastle Sports Ground
Newcastle: L. Milne (Maitland), J. Bradley (South), R. Duncan (Kurri), F. Threlfo (Maitland), B. Carlson (North), L. Brown (Maitland), E. Long (North), C. Gill (North), J. Gordon (Waratah), J. Evans (Maitland), A. Paul (Lakes), D. Schofield (Cessnock), B. Haslam (Central).
France: André, Contrastin, Merquey, Comes, Cantoni, Bellan, Caillou (c), Rinaldi, Audoubert, Mazon, Montrucolis, Delaye, Perez.
Referee: H. Gillard. Touch judges: G. Hamilton & W. Wheatley.
France: T: Perez, Rinaldi; G: Comes 3.
Newcastle: T: Threlfo, Carlson; G: Threlfo.
Weather: good. Att. 21,480. (£3,078) KO 2.30pm.

30 May France 26 Western Districts 24

Forbes
Western Districts: O. Kennerson (Bathurst), N. Jacobson (Condobolin) (c), L. Nosworthy (Narromine), J. Birney (Coolah), M. Smith (Wellington), R. Trudgett (Wellington), W. Kelly (Lithgow); J. West (Orange), I. Walsh (Condobolin), F. Hogan (Mendooran), L. Kable (Coonabarabran), R. Kelly (Forbes), K. Slattery (Canowindra).
France: Puig-Aubert (c), Contrastin, Lespes, Bellan, André, Duffort, Dop, Rinaldi, Audoubert, Beraud, Lopez, Ponsinet, Montrucolis.
Referee: K. Rowan (Lithgow). Touch judges: A. Dowell & J. Flynn.
France: T: Beraud 2, Bellan, André; G: Puig-Aubert 7.
Western Districts: T: Trudgett 3, Birney; G: Kennerson 6.
Weather: fine/cold. Att. 5,950. (£972) KO 3.05pm.

2 June France 19 Sydney 19

Sydney Cricket Ground
Sydney: C. Churchill (South Sydney) (c), J. Bliss (Manly-Warringah), R. Thomas (Eastern Suburbs), G. Willoughby (Manly-Warringah), J. Graves (South Sydney), F. Stanmore (Western Suburbs), K. Holman (Western Suburbs), D. Donogue (South Sydney), K. Schubert (Manly-Warringah), J. Holland (St George), B. Purcell (South Sydney), N. Mulligan (St George), L. Cowie (South Sydney).
France: Puig-Aubert, Contrastin, Merquey, Comes, Cantoni, Duffort, Crespo, Bartoletti, Genoud, Mazon, Ponsinet, Genoud, Calixte.
Referee: G. Bishop. Touch judges: A. Shipway & G. Taylor.
France: T: Crespo, Cantoni, Brousse; G: Puig-Aubert 5.
Sydney: T: Willoughby 2, Mulligan; G: Graves 4, Purcell.
Weather: fine. Att. 44,522 (£5,632). KO 2.30pm.

6 June France 10 Riverina 20

Albury Sports Ground
Riverina: L. Koch (Gundagai), N. Kingsmill (Albury), B. Powdery (Boorowa), N. Bruce (Junee), J. Biscaya (Lockhart), R. McDonnell (Cootamundra), J. Scott (Young), N. Milton (Temora), P. Coupland (Albury), N. Hand (Gundagai) (c), D. Piper (Young), J. Green (Cowra), P. O'Connor (Harden-Murrumburrah).
France: Puig-Aubert, André, Bellan, Merquey, Lespes, Caillou (c), Dop, Rinaldi, Audoubert, Beraud, Delaye, Lopez, Montrucolis.
Referee: N. Hedditch (Wagga). Touch judges: N. van Every & G. Beer.
France: T: André 2; G: Puig-Aubert 2.
Riverina: T: Biscaya, O'Connor; G: Koch 7.
Weather: fine. Att. 4,129 (£563). KO 3.10pm.

11 June France 26 Australia 15

First test, Sydney Cricket Ground
Australia: C. Churchill (c) (NSW), J. Bliss (NSW), G. Willoughby (NSW), N. Hazzard (Q), J. Graves (NSW), F. Stanmore (NSW), K. Holman (NSW), D. Hall (NSW), K. Schubert (NSW), D. Donoghue (NSW), B. Davies (Q), N. Mulligan (NSW), H. Crocker (NSW).
France: Puig-Aubert (c), Contrastin, Merquey, Comes, Cantoni, Galaup, Dop, Bartoletti, Genoud, Mazon, Brousse, Ponsinet, Duffort.
Referee: T. McMahon. Touch judges: R. O'Donnell & A. Dengate.
France: T: Cantoni 2, Contrastin, Genoud; G: Puig-Aubert 7.
Australia: T: Willoughby, Crocker, Graves; G: Graves 3.
Weather: fine. Att. 60,160 (£11,268). KO 2.00pm (Monday, King's Birthday).

13 June France 29 Northern Division 12

Armidale

Northern Division: K. McCrohon (Armidale), M. Murphy (Inverell), N. Young (W. Tamworth), J. Goldman (Uralla), N. Thornton (Uralla), R. Madden (Inverell), E. Fraser (Moree) (c), B. Carlton (Walcha), A. Hardman (Moree), A. Henderson (Moree), J. Glimore (Scone), B. Jackson (Moree), C. Bull (Manilla).

France: André, Lespes, Caillou (c), Crespo, Bellan, Galaup, Dop, Rinaldi, Audoubert, Beraud, Lopez, Delaye, Brousse.

Referee: R. Campbell. Touch judges: Hilton & Whitby.

France: T: Brousse 2, Delaye, Crespo, Rinaldi, Lespes, Lopez; G: Caillou 4.

Northern Division: T: Madden, Murphy; G: Fraser 3.

Weather: rain. Att. 6,000 (£809). KO 3.00pm.

16 June France 22 Queensland 22

The Gabba, Brisbane

Queensland: N. Linde (Ipswich), D. Flannery (Ipswich), N. Hazzard (Bundaberg), R. McGlynn (Bundaberg), D. McGovern (Toowoomba), H. Griffiths (Ipswich), K. McCaffery (Toowoomba), D. Hall (Toowoomba) (c), R. Davis (Mackay), A. Thompson (Brisbane), B. Drew (Bundaberg), B. Davies (Brisbane), H. Crocker (Brisbane).

France: Puig-Aubert (c), Contrastin, Merquey, Galaup, Cantoni, Duffort, Crespo, Bartoletti, Genoud, Beraud, Delaye, Ponsinet, Mazon.

Referee: J. Hoffman (Ipswich). Touch judges: G. Gray & T. Hempenstall.

France: T: Crespo, Cantoni, Genoud, Contrastin; G: Puig-Aubert 5.

Queensland: T: McGovern, Flannery, Thompson, Crocker; G: Linde 5.

Weather: fine. Att. 25,867 (£4,015). KO 2.15pm.

19 June France 38 Central Queensland 14

Rockhampton

Central Queensland: A. Poole (Rockhampton), S. Irvine (Blackall), M. Hauff (Blackall), W. Gill (Barcaldine), L. Jeffcoat (Rockhampton), M. Irwin (Blackall), B. Johnson (Longreach), M. Turnbull (Blackall), H. Johnson (Rockhampton), C. Harkin (Rockhampton), R. Beath (Rockhampton), N. Elliott (Winton), T. Whitehead (Rockhampton).

France: Puig-Aubert (c), Cantoni, André, Comes, Lespes, Bellan, Duffort, Beraud, Audoubert, Rinaldi, Montrucolis, Lopez, Calixte.

Referee: H. Gilbert. Touch judges: D. McGuirk & J. Tryhorn.

France: T: Comes 2, Audoubert, Lespes, Cantoni, Duffort, Beraud, Puig-Aubert; G: Puig-Aubert 6, Comes.

Central Queensland: T: Harkin, Irvine; G: Gill 2, Beath, B. Johnson.

Weather: fine. Att. 4,598 (£1,119). KO 3.30pm.

24 June France 50 North Queensland 17

Townsville

North Queensland: J. Jabore (Mackay), T. Boland (Cairns), J. Horrigan (Ayr) (c), F. Power (Cairns), G. Farrelly (Cairns), R. Banks (C. Towers), M. Short (Townsville), C. Woods (Ayr), J. Wedesweiler (Mackay), H. Ronald (Mackay), H. Robertson (Townsville), R. Greenwood (Mackay), R. McLennan (Ayr).

France: Puig-Aubert (c), Contrastin, Comes, Crespo, Cantoni, Merquey, Galaup, Bartoletti, Genoud, Mazon, Montrucolis, Ponsinet, Duffort.

Referee: W. Morrison. Touch judges: R. Allison & H. Roberts.

France: T: Contrastin 3, Cantoni 2, Montrucolis 2, Comes, Crespo, Galaup, Bartoletti, Ponsinet; G: Puig-Aubert 6, Comes.

North Queensland: T: Short 2, Horrigan; G: Farrelly 4.

Weather: warm. Att. 11,000 (£2,449) both records. KO 3pm.

27 June France 44 Wide Bay 19

Bundaberg

Wide Bay: K. Kennedy (Maryborough), M. Tickle (Gympie), E. Barnes (Bundaberg), R. McGlynn (Bundaberg) (c), K. Gayton (Bundaberg), D. Nixon (Bundaberg), N. Adsett (Nambour), I. Lloyd-Jones (Bundaberg), D. Jackwitz (Bundaberg), M. Kasmer (Bundaberg), B. Long (Gympie), T. Hooper (Nambour), K. Kendrick (Maryborough).

France: Galaup, André, Bellan, Montrucolis, Lespes, Caillou (c), Dop, Martin, Audoubert, Beraud, Delaye, Rinaldi, Lopez.

Referee: S.W. Chambers. Touch judges: E. Paten & C. Cunningham.

France: T: André 3, Martin 2, Bellan, Caillou, Audoubert, Dop, Rinaldi; G: Caillou 7.

Wide Bay: T: Lloyd-Jones, Hooper, Jackwitz, Adsett, Nixon; G: Lloyd-Jones 2.
Weather: fine. Att. 4,500 (£666). KO 2.30pm.

30 June France 11 Australia 23
Second test: The Gabba, Brisbane
Australia: C. Churchill (c) (NSW), D. Flannery (Q), N. Hazzard (Q), C. Geelan (NSW), N. Pidding (NSW), F. Stanmore (NSW), K. Holman (NSW), D. Hall (Q), E. Hammerton (NSW), A. Thompson (Q), B. Drew (Q), B. Davies (Q), H. Crocker (NSW).
France: Puig-Aubert (c), Contrastin, Crespo, Comes, Cantoni, Merquey, Dop, Bartoletti, Genoud, Mazon, Brousse, Ponsinet, Duffort.
Referee: T. McMahon (NSW). Touch judges: V. Lynagh & T. Hempenstall.
France: T: Merquey; G: Puig-Aubert 4.
Australia: T: Holman, Flannery, Hall; G: Pidding 6, Churchill 1 (dg).
Weather: fine. Att. 35,000 (capacity) Receipts £8,952 (record). KO 2.30pm.

3 July France 17 Brisbane 16
The Gabba, Brisbane
Brisbane: N. Pope (Valley), W. McDonald (Western Suburbs), A. Watson (Western Suburbs), N. Wilson (Souths), R. Kille (Easts), G. Atherden (Norths) (c), R. Stanton (Easts), W. Sims (Western Suburbs), T. Coman (Brothers), K. Blackford (Wynnum), J. Fallon (Brothers), B. Davies (Brothers), H. Crocker (Souths).
France: Puig-Aubert, André, Lopez, Bellan, Lespes, Galaup, Caillou, Beraud, Audoubert, Martin, Rinaldi, Delaye, Montrucolis.
Referee: V. Lynagh. Touch judges: T. Hempenstall & M. Thompson.
France: T: Lespes, Galaup, Puig-Aubert; G: Puig-Aubert 4.
Brisbane: T: McDonald, Atherden; G: Pope 5.
Weather: fine. Att. 10,750 (£1,744). KO 3.30pm.

7 July France 20 Toowoomba 17
Toowoomba
Toowoomba: W. Sullivan, P. McMahon, A. Halpin, S. Hunter, M. Higgins, J. Heidke, K. McCaffery, D. Hall, K. Boshammer, J. Rooney, W. Beardsworth, G. Teys, R. Teys.
France: Puig-Aubert (c), Lespes, Merquey, Duffort, Cantoni, Galaup, Crespo, Genoud, Martin, Bartoletti, Rinaldi, Brousse, Montrucolis.
Referee: H. Reithmuller. Touch judges: F. Russell & N. Castley.
France: T: Crespo 2, Cantoni, Merquey; G: Puig-Aubert 4.
Toowoomba: T: G. Teys, McMahon, Higgins; G: McCaffery 4.
Weather: fine. Att. 10,939 (£2,197). KO 2.30pm.

11 July France 33 North Coast 9
Lismore
North Coast: A. Lawson (Coffs Harbour), K. McDonald (Taree), C. Sherwood (Tweed), A. Duncan (Bowraville), R. Algie (Taree), A. White (Taree) (c), E. Carney (Wauchope), B. Cook (Taree), K. McKiernan (Kempsey), R. Campbell (Bowraville), R. Chaffer (Macksville), G. Alaban (Macksville), K. Killett (Macksville).
France: Puig-Aubert, Contrastin, Caillou (c), Bellan, Lespes, Galaup, Dop, Beraud, Audoubert, Mazon, Lopez, Brousse, Perez.
Referee: F. McGuigan. Touch judges: G. Tarrant & A. Barrow.
France: T: Brousse 2, Caillou 2, Puig-Aubert, Bellan, Lopez; G: Puig-Aubert 6.
North Coast: T: R. Cook; G: Lawson 2, White.
Weather: good. Att. 8,710 (£1,142). KO 3.05pm.

14 July France 14 New South Wales 14
Sydney Cricket Ground
NSW: C. Churchill (South Sydney) (c), N. Pidding (St George), J. Hawke (St George), C. Cooper (Canterbury-Bankstown), R. Roberts (St George), W. O'Connell (Manly-Warringah), K. Holman (W. Suburbs), F. Brown (Manly-Warringah), K. Schubert (Manly-Warringah), D. Donoghue (South Sydney), N. Mulligan (St George), C. Banks (E. Suburbs), L. Cowie (S. Sydney).
France: Puig-Aubert (c), Contrastin, Merquey, Comes, Cantoni, Galaup, Crespo, Bartoletti, Martin, Mazon, Brousse, Ponsinet, Duffort.
Referee: J. O'Brien. Touch Judges: R. Cummins & J. Kelly.
France: G: Puig-Aubert 7.
NSW: T: O'Connell, Brown; G: Pidding 4.
Weather: good. Att. 45,579 (£5,928). KO 2.30pm.

15 July France 24 Southern Division 13

Wollongong
Southern Division: R. Thomas (Wollongong), T. Cook (CBC Wollongong), J. Seymour (Bowral), L. Torpy (Wollongong), A. Thompson (Nowra), J. Rouse, J. McDonald (Kiama), W. Burgess (Wollongong), W. Bolt (CBC Wollongong), J. Ralston (Port Kembla), A. Miller (Berry), B. Smith (Thirroul) (c), D. Townsend (Port Kembla).
France: Comes, Perez, Bellan, Duffort, Lespes, Caillou (c), Dop, Bartoletti, Audoubert, Beraud, Delaye, Lopez, Montrucolis.
Referee: A. Grew. Touch judges: A. Kean & K. Macrae.
France: T: Caillou, Audoubert, Beraud, Delaye; G: Lopez 3, Comes 3.
Southern Division: T: Seymour; G: Smith 3, McDonald 2.
Weather: showery. Att. 11,334 (£1,585). KO 2.45pm.

21 July France 35 Australia 14

Third test: Sydney Cricket Ground
Australia: C. Churchill (NSW) (c), D. Flannery (Q), N. Hazzard (Q), J. Hawke (NSW), N. Pidding (NSW), W. O'Connell, K. Holman (NSW), D. Donoghue (NSW), K. Schubert (NSW), D. Hall (Q), B. Drew (Q), B. Davies (Q), H. Crocker (NSW).
France: Puig-Aubert (c), Contrastin, Merquey, Comes, Cantoni, Duffort, Crespo, Bartoletti, Genoud, Mazon, Brousse, Ponsinet, Calixte.
Referee: T. McMahon. Touch judges: G. Taylor & A. Shipway.
France: T: Crespo 3, Contrastin 2, Comes, Brousse; G: Puig-Aubert 7.
Australia: T: Hall, Davies; G: Pidding 4.
Weather: perfect. Att. 67,009 (record). Receipts £11,493. KO 2.00pm.

15 August France 11 NSW XIII 29

Sydney Cricket Ground)
NSW XIII: R. Willey (Canterbury-Bankstown), J. Lumsden (Manly-Warringah), G. Willoughby (Manly-Warringah), M. McCoy (St George), J. McClean (North Sydney), G. Hawick (South Sydney), C. Donohoe (Eastern Suburbs), B. Orrock (South Sydney), K. Schubert (Manly-Warringah), F. Brown (Manly-Warringah), F. Ashton (Eastern Suburbs), J. Rayner (South Sydney) (c), N. Charlton (Canterbury-Bankstown).
France: Puig-Aubert (c), Contrastin, Crespo, Bellan, Cantoni, Galaup, Dop, Beraud, Martin, Mazon, Brousse, Ponsinet, Calixte.
Referee: J. O'Brien. Touch judges: D. Nicholson & T. Bellew.
France: T: Cantoni; G: Puig-Aubert 4.
NSW XIII: T: Orrock, Charlton, Ashton, Willoughby, Lumsden; G: Willey 6, Lumsden.
Weather: fine. Att. 29,304 (£4,037). KO 3.30pm.

18 August France 34 Australian XIII 17

Melbourne Showground
Australian XIII: C. Churchill (NSW) (c), W. Dickason (Vic), K. Woolfe (NSW), N. Hazzard (Q), J. McClean (NSW), G. Hawick (NSW), K. McCaffery (Q), J. Balmain (Vic), E. Hammerton (NSW), G. Teys (Q), B. Davies (Q), J. Rayner (NSW), H. Crocker (Q).
France: Puig-Aubert, André, Crespo, Caillou (c), Contrastin, Bellan, Calixte, Perez, Martin, Audoubert, Ponsinet, Brousse, Calixte.
Referee: J. Davies. Touch judges: S. Coleman & E. Brown.
France: T: Beraud 2, Contrastin, André, Caillou, Puig-Aubert; G: Puig-Aubert 8.
Australian XIII: T: McCaffery, Davies, Balmain; G: McCaffery 2, Churchill, Woolfe.
Weather: rainy. Att. 4,460 (£856). KO 3.00pm.

26 August France 70 Western Australia 23

Claremont Showground, Perth
Western Australia: J. McGuinness, R. Sampson, N. Plester, W. Nicholson, R. Quinlan, S. Saxon, L. Leavy, G. Vooles, K. Allen, R. Robinson, J. Stewart, R. Patching, F. Sullivan (c).
France: Puig-Aubert, Cantoni, Crespo, André, Contrastin, Caillou (c), Dop, Beraud, Martin, Audoubert, Brousse, Ponsinet, Calixte.
Referee: H. W. Fisher. Touch judges: N. Stolberg & R. Utting.
France: T: Cantoni 3, Beraud 2, Puig-Aubert 2, Caillou, Contrastin, André, Audoubert, Brousse, Ponsinet, Martin, Calixte, Crespo; G: Puig-Aubert 7, Calixte 2, Contrastin, Cantoni.
Western Australia: T: Quinlan 2, Stewart; G: Sampson 7.
Weather: perfect. Att. 14,500 (£1,070 by sale of badges). KO 3.20pm.

124

Individual playing records in Australia

Player	Tests	Others	T	G	Pts.
Puig-Aubert	3	14	6	96	210
V. Cantoni	3	9	12	1	38
R. Constrastin	3	11	10	2	34
G. Comes	3	7	6	7	32
J. Merquey	3	7	2	0	6
R. Duffort	3	8	1	0	3
E. Brousse	3	9	6	0	18
E. Ponsinet	3	8	2	0	6
G. Genoud	3	5	4	0	12
L. Mazon	3	7	0	0	0
P. Bartoletti	3	7	1	0	3
J. Dop	2	9	1	0	3
J. Crespo	2	9	10	0	30
G. Calixte	1	6	1	2	7
G. Galaup	1	9	2	0	6
R. Caillou	0	10	6	11	40
A. Beraud	0	13	8	0	24
O. Lespes	0	10	3	0	9
M. André	0	11	9	0	27
M. Bellan	0	10	3	0	9
M. Lopez	0	9	4	4	20
F. Montrucolis	0	9	2	0	6
F. Rinaldi	0	8	3	0	9
A. Audoubert	0	11	4	0	12
M. Martin	0	7	3	0	9
G. Delaye	0	7	2	0	6
R. Perez	0	4	1	0	3
Totals			**112**	**123**	**582**

1951 New Zealand match details

25 July France 5 West Coast 2
Wingham Park, Greymouth
West Coast: R. Nuttall, C. McGougan, J. Forrest, A. Campbell, G. Menzies, R. Wright, G. H. Ord, J. Newton, R. Aynsley, F. Malloy, C. McBride, F. Mulcare, R. Neilson.
France: Comes, Cantoni, Caillou, Galaup, Merquey, Duffort, Crespo, Audoubert, Martin, Bartoletti, Lopez, Delaye, Montrucolis.
France: T: Comes; G: Caillou.
West Coast: G: Nuttall.
Weather: rainy. Att.3,667. Referee: J. Griffin.

28 July France 13 Canterbury 7
Christchurch
Canterbury: K. Henry, W. McKenzie, G. Neiman, C. Paskell, B. Stapley, S. Parkes, J. Haig, I. Pimley, L. Blanchard, J. Bond, J. Curtain, J. Crofts, A. Atkinson.
France: Comes, Lespes, Caillou, Bellan, Contrastin, Duffort and Dop, Mazon, Martin, Beraud, Ponsinet, Montrucolis, Perez.
France: T: Caillou, Beraud, Contrastin; G: Comes 2.
Canterbury: T: Paskell; G: Bond, Haig.
Weather: wet/windy. Att. 6,990.

30 July France 26 Wellington 13
Basin Reserve, Wellington
Wellington: F. Mott, K. McButler, J. Dodd, M. Church, H. McCarthy, J. Keen, T. McPherson, W. Greyl, R. Bolton, K. English, K. Meates, R. Paratene, L. Morgan.
France: Dop, Cantoni, Comes, Merquey, Contrastin, Caillou, Crespo, Mazon, Martin, Lopez, Brousse, Beraud, Montrucolis.
France: T: Beraud 2, Mazon 2, Lopez, Dop; G: Lopez 2, Mazon 2.
Wellington: T: English; G: Mott 3, Church 2.
Weather: perfect. Att.8,602 (Monday afternoon in rugby union stronghold)

4 August France 15 New Zealand 16

Test match: Carlaw Park, Auckland
New Zealand: D. White, J. Forrest, T. Baxter, M. Robertson (c), B. Hough, G. Menzies, J. Haigh, K. English, G. Davidson, C. Johnson, D. Richards-Jolly, C. McBride, T. Hardwick.
France: Puig-Aubert (c), Contrastin, Comes, Merquey, Cantoni, Duffort, Crespo, Mazon, Martin, Bartoletti, Brousse, Ponsinet, Montrucolis.
France: T: Cantoni 2, Ponsinet; G: Puig-Aubert 3.
New Zealand: T: Menzies, Baxter; G: White 5.
Referee: J. Griffiths (West Coast). Att. 19,229 (£5,000).

6 August France 15 Auckland 10

Carlaw Park, Auckland
Auckland: D. White, J. Edwards, T. Baxter, C. Eastlake, W. Hough, B. Robertson, D. Barchard, C. Johnson, G. Davidson, R. Cranch, D. Richards-Jolley, C. Hurndell, A. Wiles.
France: Puig-Aubert, Lespes, André, Galaup, Crespo, Caillou (c), Dop, Beraud, Martin, Audoubert, Brousse, Ponsinet, Duffort.
France: T: Brousse, Martin, Puig-Aubert; G: Puig-Aubert 3.
Auckland: T: Johnson, Hough; G: White 2.
Referee: G. Kelly. Att. 20,414.

9 August France 25 South Auckland 7

Hamilton
South Auckland: Pearson, O'Callaghan, Smith, Parsonage, Carrigan, Seddon, Oake, Hambleton, Dow, Rogers, Moyce, Williams, Hardwick (c).
France: Puig-Aubert, Cantoni, Bellan, Crespo, Contrastin, Galaup, Dop, Beraud, Auduobert, Genoud, Bartoletti, Brousse, Calixte.
France: T: Cantoni, Contrastin, Brousse, Galaup, Crespo; G: Puig-Aubert 3, Cantoni, Bartoletti.
South Auckland: T: Smith; G: Hardwick 2.
Referee: G. Avery. Att. 7,480.

11 August France 23 Taranaki 7

Pukekura Park, New Plymouth
Taranaki: B. Lambert, P. Barton, R. Watson, R. McKay, C. Hawkins, R. McCullock, P. Dymond, A. McCleod, L. Murray, R. Edwards, P. White, C. Martin, M. Casperson.
France: Puig-Aubert, André, Bellan, Caillou, Cantoni, Calixte, Dop, Audoubert, Martin, Bartoletti, Beraud, Lopez, Perez.
France: T; Cantoni, Beraud, Martin, Bartoletti, Dop, André, Puig-Aubert; G: Puig-Aubert.
Taranaki: T; Casperson; G: McKay, McCullock.
Att. 6,473.

Individual playing records in New Zealand

Player	Tests	Others	T	G	Pts.
Puig-Aubert	1	3	2	10	26
V. Cantoni	1	4	4	1	14
R. Constrastin	1	3	2	0	6
G. Comes	1	3	1	2	7
J. Merquey	1	2	0	0	0
R. Duffort	1	3	0	0	0
E. Brousse	1	3	2	0	6
E. Ponsinet	1	2	1	0	3
G. Genoud	0	1	0	0	0
L. Mazon	1	2	2	2	10
P. Bartoletti	1	3	1	1	5
J. Dop	0	5	2	0	6
J. Crespo	1	4	1	0	3
G. Calixte	0	2	0	0	0
G. Galaup	0	3	1	0	3
R. Caillou	0	5	1	1	5
A. Beraud	0	5	4	0	12
O. Lespes	0	2	0	0	0
M. André	0	2	1	0	3
M. Bellan	0	3	0	0	0
M. Lopez	0	3	1	2	7
F. Montrucolis	1	3	0	0	0

F. Rinaldi	0	0	0	0	0
A. Audoubert	0	4	0	0	0
M. Martin	1	5	2	0	6
G. Delaye	0	1	0	0	0
R. Perez	0	2	0	0	0
Totals			**28**	**19**	**122**

1951 Complete individual playing records

Player	Tests	Others	T	G	Pts.
Puig Aubert	4	17	8	106	236
V. Cantoni	4	13	16	2	52
R. Constrastin	4	14	12	2	40
G. Comes	4	10	7	9	39
J. Merquey	4	9	2	0	6
R. Duffort	4	11	1	0	3
E. Brousse	4	12	9	0	27
E. Ponsinet	4	10	3	0	9
G. Genoud	3	6	3	0	9
L. Mazon	4	9	2	2	10
P. Bartoletti	4	10	2	1	8
J. Dop	2	14	3	0	9
J. Crespo	3	13	11	0	33
G. Calixte	1	8	1	2	7
G. Galaup	1	12	3	0	9
R. Caillou	0	15	7	12	45
A. Beraud	0	18	12	0	36
O. Lespes	0	12	3	0	9
M. André	0	12	10	0	30
M. Bellan	0	14	3	0	9
M. Lopez	0	12	5	6	27
F. Montrucolis	1	12	2	0	6
F. Rinaldi	0	8	3	0	9
A. Audoubert	0	15	4	0	12
M. Martin	1	12	5	0	15
G. Delaye	0	8	2	0	6
R. Perez	0	6	1	0	3
Totals			**140**	**142**	**704**

1955: Second French tour

Australia

15 May	W	France 31 Western Australia 6 (Perth)
18 May	W	France 48 South Australia 10 (Adelaide)
21 May	W	France 44 Victoria 2 (Melbourne)
25 May	L	France 3 Monaro 11 (Canberra)
28 May	L	France 0 Sydney 25 (Sydney)
1 June	L	France 27 Riverina 29 (Narrandera)
4 June	L	France 24 NSW 29 (Sydney)
5 June	L	France 9 Southern Division 16 (Wollongong)
11 June	**L**	**France 8 Australia 20 (Sydney)**
13 June	W	France 21 Brisbane 11 (Brisbane)
15 June	L	France 6 Toowoomba 35 (Toowoomba)
18 June	W	France 23 Queensland 17 (Brisbane)
19 June	W	France 40 Central Queensland 24 (Rockhampton)
21 June	W	France 29 Western Queensland 14 (Barcaldine)
25 June	W	France 66 Far North Queensland 21 (Cairns)
26 June	W	France 42 North Queensland 26 (Townsville)
29 June	L	France 17 Northern Division 18 (Casino)
2 July	**W**	**France 29 Australia 28 (Brisbane)**
3 July	W	France 46 Wide Bay 17 (Gympie)
5 July	W	France 19 Ipswich 10 (Ipswich)

9 July   L   France 15 Newcastle 17 (Newcastle)
13 July   W   France 28 Sydney Colts 26 (Sydney)
16 July   L   France 23 NSW 37 (Sydney)
20 July   W   France 11 Western Division 8 (Parkes)
23 July   W   France 8 Australia 5 (Sydney)

Played 25, won 15, drawn 0, lost 10. Points: F 617, A: 462.

New Zealand

27 July   W   France 18 West Coast 12 (Greymouth)
30 July   L   France 13 Canterbury 24 (Christchurch)
2 August   W   France 19 Wellington 14 (Wellington)
4 August   W   France 46 Taranaki 17 (New Plymouth)
6 August   W   France 19 New Zealand 9 (Auckland)
10 August   L   France 20 Maoris 28 (Wellington)
13 August   L   France 6 New Zealand 11 (Auckland)
15 August   L   France 15 Auckland 17 (Auckland)

Played 8, won 4, drawn 0, lost 4. Points: F: 156, A: 132.

Played 33, won 19, drawn 0, lost 14. Points: F: 773, A: 594.

1955 Australian match details

15 May France 31 Western Australia 6
Belmont Stadium, Perth
W. Australia: Williams, R. Williams, Wells, Quinlan, Plester, O'Brien, Dickhart, Kennedy, Robson, Carr, Bowler, Cahill, Hillier.
France: Dop (c), Ducasse, Duplé, Larroudé, Contrastin, Jiminez, Levy, Carrère, Moulis, Berthomieu, Delaye, Pambrun, Save.
Referee: R. Utting. Touch judges: K. Allen & R. Dix.
France: T; Contrastin 3, Save 3, Ducasse 2, Duplé; G: Save 2.
W. Australia: T: Wells, O'Brien.
Weather: perfect. Att.15,000 (record) (£1,307) KO 3.15pm.

18 May France 48 South Australia 10
Norwood Oval, Adelaide
S. Australia: Chadwick (c), Merritt, Lewis, Beythien, Mullins, Foster, Jennings, Brain, Duncan, Pryor, Mulvey, Hanson, Nelson.
France: Dop (c), Savonne, Larroudé, Duplé, Cantoni, Jiminez, Levy, Berthomieu, Moulis, Carrère, Fabre, Delaye, Save.
Referee: A. Burns. Touch judges: L. Dangerfield & G. Tavener.
France: T: Savonne 3, Cantoni 3, Dop 2, Moulis, Carrère, Duplé, Jiminez; G: Moulis 4, Duplé 2.
S. Australia: T: Jennings 2 (1 penalty); G: Nelson 2.
Weather: cold. Att.1074. (£161). KO 8.20pm.

21 May France 44 Victoria 2
Richmond CG, Melbourne
Victoria: Jones, Borton, Axelson, Isles, Summerfield, Denman, Robinson, Hanley, Beach, Whitley, Judd, Holden, Dauth (c).
France: Dop (c), Ducasse, Duplé, Larroudé, Contrastin, Jiminez, Levy, Carrère, Moulis, Barthomieu, Fabre, Delaye, Save.
Referee: T. O'Connor. Touch judges: N. Jahnke & D. Walsh.
France: T: Duplé 2, Ducasse 2, Larroudé 2, Moulis 2, Save, Delaye, Contrastin, Jiminez; G: Moulis 2, Jiminez, Save.
Victoria: G: Dauth.
Weather: dull. Att.2,311 (£360). KO 3.00pm.

25 May France 3 Monaro 11
Manuka Oval, Canberra
Monaro: Johnson (Cooma), Grieves (Yass), Corey (Captain's Flat), Brogan (Cooma), Elliot (Bombala), Bennett (Crookwell), Liege (Bombala), Rayner (Yass), Quinliven (Canberra), Moon (Cooma), Yelds (Bombala), Glover (Binalong), Fields (Yass).

France: Dop (c), Contrastin, Duplé, Larroudé, Ducasse, Jiminez, Levy, Berthomieu, Moulis, Fabre, Delaye, Pambrun, Save.
Referee: H. Gillard. Touch judges: J. McKie & K. Gibb.
France T: Barthomieu.
Monaro T: Elliott; G: Brogan 3, Bennett.
Weather: cloudy. Att. 4,000 (£680). KO 3.15pm.

28 May France 0 Sydney 25
Sydney Cricket Ground
Sydney: Slade (Parramatta) (c), Kite (St George), Lees (St George), Hawick (Souths), Pidding (Easts), Duncan (Manly-Warringah), Donohoe (Souths), Orrock (St George), Kearney (St George), Bull (Manly-Warringah), Holloway (Newtown), Jackson (Manly-Warringah), Diversi (Norths).
France: Benausse, Voron, Teisseire, Merquey (c), Savonne, Jiminez, Guilhem, Vanel, Audoubert, Fabre, Pambrun, Delaye, Montrucolis.
Referee: J. O'Brien. Touch judges: E. Lindsay & T. Leffler.
Sydney T: Lees 2, Hawick, Orrock, Holloway; G: Pidding 5.
Weather: wet. Att. 39,445. (£5,490). KO 3.00pm.

1 June France 27 Riverina 29
Narrandera
Riverina: McGrath (Temora), Smailles (Harden), Garvin (Young), Ratcliff (West Wyalong), Kane (Barmedman), Staunton (Wagga), Cameron (Young), Slavin (Cootamundra), McDonald (Barmedman), Lynch (Leeton), Gordon (Barmedman), Moses (Griffith), Paul (Griffith).
France: Benausse, Cantoni, Larroudé, Rey, Ducasse, Delpoux, Levy, Berthomieu, Moulis, Carrère, Jammes, Save, Duplé.
Referee: J. Lane (Newcastle). Touch judges: M. Brentnall & N. Cummings.
France T: Ducasse 2, Levy, Cantoni, Larroudé; G: Benausse 6.
Riverina T: Ratcliff, Slavin, Kane; G: McGrath 10.
Weather: fine. Att. 10,000. (£1,455). KO 3.00pm.

4 June France 24 New South Wales 29
Sydney Cricket Ground
NSW: Churchill (Souths) (c), Kite (St George), Wells (Wollongong), Hawick (Souths), Adams (Maitland), Henry (Forbes), Holman (Wests), Orrock (St George), Kearney (St George), Bull (Manly-Warringah), Holloway (Newtown), Jackson (Manly-Warringah), Diversi (Norths).
France: Dop, Voron, Merquey (capt.), Rey, Ducasse, Jiminez, Levy, Berthomieu, Moulis, Vanel, Pambrun, Delaye, Duplé.
Referee: D. Lawler. Touch judges: G. Taylor & J. Kelly.
France T: Merquey 2, Ducasse, Vanel; G: Duplé 6.
NSW T: Henry 2, Adams 2, Kite, Jackson, Diversi; G: Hawick 2, Holman, Churchill.
Weather: fine. Att. 50,488. (£7,037). KO 3.00pm.

5 June France 9 Southern Division 16
Wollongong
Wollongong: Wynne (Corrimal), Morgan (Bowral), Sinclair (Campbelltown), Graham (Dapto), Morrissey (Berry), Rouse (Nowra), Dunn (Camden), Noble (Jamberoo), Delaney (Corrimal), Hodges (Wollongong), Quinn (Gerringong), Miller (Berry), Mulligan (Port Kembla) (c).
France: Jiminez, Voron, Merquey (c), Rey, Savonne, Delpoux and Dop, Carrère, Audoubert, Fabre, Delaye, Save, Duplé.
Referee: E. McIlhatton. Touch judges: A. Grew & W. Grugan.
France T: Voron; G: Duplé 3.
Southern Division T: Noble 2; G: Wynne 4, Morrissey.
Weather: rain. Att. 6,500. (£1,204). KO 3.00pm.

11 June France 8 Australia 20
First test, Sydney Cricket Ground
Australia: C. Churchill (NSW) (c), D. Flannery (Q), H. Wells (NSW), A. Watson (Q), R. Kite (NSW), D. Henry (NSW), K. Holman (NSW), D. Hall (Q), K. Kearney (NSW), R. Bull (NSW), H. Holloway (NSW), B. Davies (Q), P. Diversi (NSW).
France: Benausse, Ducasse, Merquey (capt.), Rey, Voron, Jiminez, Dop, Berthomieu, Moulis, Vanel, Delaye, Pambrun, Duplé.
Referee: D. Lawler. Touch judges: G. Taylor & J. Kelly.
France T: Ducasse, Berthomieu; G: Duplé.

Australia T: Holman 2, Wells, Kite; G: Davies 3, Holman.
Weather: fine. Att. 67,748. (£21,693). KO 3.00pm.

13 June France 21 Brisbane 11

Exhibition Ground, Brisbane
Brisbane: Pope, Pyers, Mulgrew, Watson, Mundt, McIntosh, Edwards, Plater, Hornery, Hall (c), Davies, McFadden, Wyvill.
France: Jiminez, Contrastin, Delpoux, Rey, Cantoni, Benausse, Menichelli, Vanel. Audoubert, Montrucolis (c), Save, Jammes, Levy.
Referee: J. Casey. Touch judges: J. Wallace & H. Albert.
France T: Contrastin 2, Save, Cantoni, Delpoux; G: Benausse 3.
Brisbane T: Pyers; G: Pope 4.
Weather: fine. Att. 30,000. (£3,732). KO 8.00pm.

15 June France 6 Toowoomba 35

Toowoomba
Toowoomba: Halpin, Monkland, Brown, Payne, McMahon, Laird, Hunter (c), Proudfoot, Boshammer, Teys, Duncan, Smith, Doyle.
France: Dop, Contrastin, Merquey (c), Larroudé, Cantoni, Delpoux, Guilhem, Audoubert, Moulis, Carrère, Save, Pambrun, Montrucolis.
Referee: C. Wright. Touch judges: V. Vercoe & N. Castley.
France T: Carrere 2.
Toowoomba T: Payne 2, Duncan 2, Brown, Smith, McMahon; G: Teys 6, Doyle.
Weather: showery. Att. 7,305 (all-ticket) (£1,890). KO 3.00pm.

18 June France 23 Queensland 17

The Gabba, Brisbane
Queensland: Pope, Ryan, Laird, Watson, Brown, Brennan, Connell, Davies, Hornery, Hall (c), Furner, Drew, Tyquin.
France: Dop, Contrastin, Merquey (c), Rey, Ducasse, Benausse, Menichelli, Audoubert, Moulis, Vanel, Montrucolis, Pambrun, Duplé.
Referee: J. Casey. Touch judges: H. Reithmuller & N. Kelly.
France T: Rey 2, Merquey 2, Benausse; G: Benausse 4.
Queensland T: Drew, Laird, Connell; G: Pope 4.
Weather: rain. Att. 14,871 (£2,623). KO 3.00pm.

19 June France 40 Central Queensland 24

Rockhampton
Central Queensland: Preston, Ryan, Cooper, Little, Jackson, Geelan, Connell, Hughes, Lee, Sorley, Guthridge, Sear, Watt.
France: Dop, Ducasse, Rey, Larroudé, Levy, Benausse, Menichelli, Carrère, Moulis, Vanel, Berthomieu, Montrucolis, Save.
Referee: P. Mahoney (Townsville). Touch judges: R. Tait & N. Daniells.
France T: Levy 2, Save, Berthomieu, Larroudé, Benausse, Ducasse, Carrere;
G: Benausse 8.
C. Queensland T: Connell 2, Ryan 2; G: Preston 6.
Weather: fine. Att. 7,500. (£1,626). KO 3.30pm.

21 June France 29 Central Western Queensland 14

Barcaldine
Central Western Queensland: Locke, Lehane, Barnes, Lawrence, Alexander, O'Connell, Buchester, Turnbull, Wilkinson, Maher, Nolan, Probert, Eggmolesse.
France: Benausse, Cantoni, Larroudé, Merquey (c), Voron, Delpoux, Levy, Berthomieu, Moulis, Audoubert, Jammes, Pambrun, Duplé.
Referee: P. Mahoney (Townsville). Touch judges: J. Grant & J. Steele.
France T: Pambrun 2, Larroudé 2, Benausse, Voron, Delpoux; G: Duplé 2, Benausse 2.
CW Queensland T: Turnbull, Proberts; G: Locke 2, O'Connell 2.
Weather: fine. Att. 2,250 (£500). KO 3.15pm.

25 June France 66 Far North Queensland 21

Cairns
Far North Queensland: Smith, Winklemuller, Tait, McFarlane, Christensen, Flynn, Lesina, Jager, Griffiths (c), Kratzman, Goldfinch, Greenwood, Sestero.
France: Dop, Cantoni, Rey, Levy, Larroudé, Benausse, Menichelli, Audoubert, Moulis, Vanel, Berthomieu, Carrère, Delpoux.

Referee: H. Gilbert (Rockhampton).
France T: Cantoni 3, Delpoux 3, Larroudé 2, Rey 2, Vanel, Audoubert, Levy, Carrère;
G: Benausse 12.
Far North Queensland T: Christiensen 2, Kratzman, Winklemuller, Greenwood; G: Smith 3.
Weather: fine. Att. 5,943 (£1,747) KO 3pm.

26 June France 42 North Queensland 26
Townsville
N Queensland: Hoyle, Roberts, Blaik, Ford, McDonald, Backer, Doonan, Clifford, Fuller, Ellery, Ronald, Brereton, Farquhar.
France: Dop, Voron, Rey, Merquey (c), Ducasse, Benausse, Tesseire, Jammes, Moulis, Carrère, Save, Duplé, Montrucolis.
Referee: H. Gilbert. Touch judges: K. Brennan & J. Rolls.
France T: Ducasse 2, Voron 2, Teisseire 2, Dop, Benausse; G: Benausse 9.
North Queensland T: Doonan, Backer, Ronald, McDonald; G: Roberts 7.
Weather: fine. Att. 7,525. (£2,138). KO 3.00pm.

29 June France 17 Northern New South Wales 18
Casino
Northern NSW: Kennedy (Warialda), Johnson, Gartner (Nambucca), Pereira (Dorrigo), Graves (Camden Haven), Stanmore (Smithtown), O'Reilly (Lismore), Lewis (Tenterfield), Hardman (Moree), Reseck (Camden Haven), McKenzie (Inverell), Cooper (Bowraville), Rankin (Macksville).
France: Jiminez, Contrastin, Larroudé, Cantoni, Savonne, Delpoux, Menichelli, Fabre, Moulis, Carrère, Jammes, Pambrun, Levy.
Referee: J. Lane (Newcastle). Touch judges: C. Hutchinson & C. McLetchie.
France T: Contrastin 2, Cantoni, Levy, Carrere; G: Cantoni.
Northern NSW T: Stanmore, Hardman; G: Graves 6.
Weather: fine. Att. 4,500. (£900).

2 July France 29 Australia 28
Second test: The Gabba, Brisbane
Australia: C. Churchill (NSW) (c), A. Watson (Q), H. Wells (NSW), K. McCaffery (Q), R. Kite (NSW), G. Laird (Q), K. Holman (NSW), D. Hall (Q), K. Kearney (NSW), R. Bull (NSW), H. Holloway (NSW), B. Davies (Q), H. Crocker (NSW).
France: Dop, Ducasse, Merquey (c), Rey, Voron, Benausse, Tesseire, Vanel, Audoubert, Montrucolis, Berthomieu, Save, Duplé.
Referee: D. Lawler. Touch judges: N. Kelly & T. Hempenstall.
France T: Rey 2, Merquey 2, Ducasse; G: Benausse 6, Duplé.
Australia T: Laird 2, Crocker 2, Kite, Holloway; G: Davies 3, Churchill, Holman.
Weather: fine. Att. 45,745. (£14,467). KO 2.45pm.

3 July France 46 Wide Bay 17
Gympie
Wide Bay: Connell, Kavanagh, McGlynn, Blanchard, Vernardos, Renshaw, Prickett, Malone, Western, Schaffverous, Zeibath, King, Drysdale.
France: Benausse, Larroudé, Rey, Jiminez, Cantoni, Delpoux and Guilhem, Montrucolis, Audoubert, Vanel, Pambrun, Jammes, Levy.
Referee: T. Hempenstall (Brisbane). Touch judges: R. Crane & C. Weinheimer.
France T: Cantoni 4, Larroudé 2, Jiminez, Montrucolis, Delpoux, Jammes;
G: Benausse 8.
Wide Bay T: Kavanagh, Renshaw, McGlynn, Prickett, Vernardos; G: Blanchard.
Weather: fine. Att. 5,391. (£1,245).

5 July France 19 Ipswich 10
Ipswich
Ipswich: Haviland, Watterson, Duncan, Doyle, Pearson, Brennan, Whybird, Beattie, Jackwitz, Parcell, Rashleigh, Drew, Meehan.
France: Benausse, Ducasse, Merquey (c), Delpoux, Cantoni, Jiminez, Menichelli, Fabre, Audoubert, Pambrun, Jammes, Berthomieu, Duplé.
Referee: N. Kelly. Touch judges: M. Morgan & B. Creedy.
France T: Cantoni 2, Ducasse; G: Benausse 5.
Ipswich T: Brennan, Parcell; G: Haviland 2.
Weather: good. Att. 4,242. (£841). KO 3.30pm.

9 July France 15 Newcastle 17

Newcastle

Newcastle: Naughton, Batey, Foley, Chapple, Adams, Banks, Sneddon, Hawke, Gibbs, Curry, Schofield, Lennard, Gray.

France: Dop, Cantoni, Rey, Jiminez, Contrastin, Benausse, Levy, Vanel, Moulis, Fabre, Montrucolis, Jammes, Duplé.

Referee: E. McIlhatton. Touch judges: R. Baker & G. McPherson.

France T: Cantoni, Contrastin, Fabre; G: Benausse 3.

Newcastle T: Curry 2, Batey 2, Hawke; G: Naughton.

Weather: fine. Att. 20,824. (£3,754). KO 2.45pm.

13 July France 28 Sydney Colts 26

Sydney Cricket Ground

Sydney Colts: Slade (Parramatta) (c), Allsop (Easts), Weekes (St George), Fifield (Balmain), O'Brien (St George), McNamara (St George), Diett (Manly-Warringah), Cameron (Parramatta), Strong (Norths), Fearnley (Easts), Jackson (Manly-Warringah), Narvo (Norths), Pert (St George).

France: Benausse, Voron, Merquey (c), Rey, Larroudé, Jiminez, Duplé, Levy, Carrère, Audoubert, Vanel, Pambrun, Save.

Referee: D. Lawler. Touch judges: B. Jackman & J. Roach.

France T: Merquey 2, Voron 2, Duplé, Vanel; G: Benausse 5.

Sydney Colts T: Cameron, Jackson, Weekes, Fifield, Allsop, Diett; G: Allsop 3, O'Brien.

Att. 13,282. (£1,783).

16 July France 23 New South Wales 37

Sydney Cricket Ground

New South Wales: Churchill (Souths) (c), Kite (St George), Wells (Wollongong), Poole (Norths), Adams (Maitland), Henry (Forbes), Holman (Wests), Marsh (Balmain), Kearney (St George), Bull (Manly-Warringah), Crocker (Parramatta), Holloway (Newtown), Diversi (Norths).

France: Dop, Cantoni, Jiminez, Merquey (c), Contrastin, Benausse, Levy, Montrucolis, Moulis, Fabre, Pambrun, Jammes, Save.

Referee: J. O'Brien. Touch judges: J. Tubridy & A. Holt.

France T: Contrastin 3, Pambrun, Fabre; G: Benausse 4.

NSW T: Kite 2, Adams 2, Holloway, Henry, Churchill; G: Churchill 8.

Att. 30,769. (£4,068).

20 July France 11 Western New South Wales 8

Parkes

Western New South Wales: Aldrich (Parkes), Hole (Condobolin), Stanford (Parkes), Bowden (Coonamble), Lawrence (Cowra), Nosworthy (Narromine), Holden (Mudgee), Hansen (Manildra), Walsh (Forbes), Border (Coonabarabran), Thurn (Orange), Perrin (Parkes), Gain (Parkes).

France: Dop, Voron, Larroudé, Cantoni, Savonne, Delpoux, Menichelli, Carrère, Mounis, Save, Jammes, Pambrun, Guilhem.

Referee: F. Ring (Wellington). Touch judges: M. Leary & T. Blacker.

France T: Voron, Carrère, Cantoni; G: Save.

Western NSW G: Aldrich 4.

Weather: good. Att. 8,306. (£1,700). KO 3.05pm.

23 July France 8 Australia 5

Third test: Sydney Cricket Ground

Australia: C. Churchill (c) (NSW), R. Kite (NSW), R. Poole (NSW), A. Watson (Q), D. Flannery (Q) , G. Laird (Q), K. Holman (NSW), R. Bull (NSW), K. Kearney (NSW), D. Hall (Q), H. Crocker (NSW), H. Holloway (NSW), B. Davies (Q).

France: Dop, Contrastin, Merquey (c), Rey, Ducasse, Benausse, Duplé, Fabre, Audoubert, Vanel, Montrucolis, Berthomieu, Levy.

Referee: J. Casey (Queensland). Touch judges: J. Kelly & G. Taylor.

France T: Contrastin, Ducasse; G: Duplé.

Australia T: Davies; G: Churchill.

Weather: fine. Att. 62,458. (£21,693). KO 2.30pm.

1955 Individual playing records in Australia

Player	Tests	Others	T	G	Pts.
G. Benausse	3	13	4	75	162
J. Dop	3	13	3	0	9
R. Contrastin	1	9	13	0	39

A. Ducasse	3	9	14	0	42
A. Savonne	0	5	3	0	9
M. Voron	2	7	7	0	21
F. Cantoni	0	13	17	1	53
J. Merquey	3	10	8	0	24
C. Teisseire	1	2	2	0	6
R. Rey	3	11	6	0	18
V. Larroudé	0	13	10	0	30
A. Jiminez	1	14	3	1	11
A. Delpoux	0	10	6	0	18
R. Guilhem	0	4	0	0	0
S. Menichelli	0	7	0	0	0
J. Audoubert	2	10	1	0	3
J. Vanel	3	9	3	0	9
J. Fabre	1	9	2	0	6
G. Delaye	1	7	1	0	3
G. Berthomieu	3	10	3	0	9
A. Carrère	0	12	7	0	21
R. Moulis	1	16	3	6	21
J. Jammes	0	10	1	0	3
J. Pambrun	1	13	3	0	9
A. Save	1	13	6	4	26
F. Montrucolis	2	9	1	0	3
C. Duplé	3	13	5	16	47
F. Levy	1	15	5	0	15
Totals			137	103	617

1955 New Zealand match details

27 July France 18 West Coast 12
Greymouth
West Coast T: Higson 2. G: McLennan 2.
France T: Savonne, Voron, Delpoux, Fabre. G: G. Benausse 3.
Att. 5,000

30 July France 12 Canterbury 24
Christchurch
Canterbury: D. Berbridge, R. Wilson, E. Anderson, I. King, C. Courtney, K. Roberts, P. Creedy, A. Atkinson, R. Turton, T. Kilkelly, J. Bond, L. Blanchard, J. Butterfield.
France: Dop, Contrastin, Larroudé, Rey, Ducasse, G. Benausse, Guilhem, Audoubert, Vanel, Montrucolis, Save, Jammes, Duplé
France T: Contrastin 2; G: Contrastin, Benausse 2.
Canterbury T: Butterfield 2, Wilson 2, Creedy, Roberts; G: Bond 2, Berbridge.
Att. 2,200.

2 August France 19 Wellington 14
Wellington
Wellington: Cunningham, Mallender, Simpson, Johansson, Scott, Fox, Dodd, Houston, Still, Kreyl, Butt, Clark, Golding.
France: Dop, Contrastin, Larroudé, Jiminez, Ducasse, Benausse, Duplé, Fabre, Audoubert, Vanel, Montrucolis, Berthomieu, Levy.
France T: Contrastin, Larroudé, Ducasse 3; G: Duplé 2.
Wellington T: Johansson, Dodd, Golding, Still; G: Scott.
Weather: rain, mud, bitterly cold. Att. 4,000.

4 August France 46 Taranaki 17
New Plymouth
France T: Voron 2, Savonne 2, Delpoux 2, Larroudé 2, Pambrun, Menichelli, F. Cantoni, Moulis; G: F. Cantoni 2, Save 2, Moulis.
Taranaki T: Tamati, McClenaghan, Hepburn; G: Savage 3, Southorn.
Weather: dry, firm. Att. 4,500.

6 August France 19 New Zealand 9
First test: Carlaw Park, Auckland
New Zealand: R. Moore, R. Hawes, R. McKay, B. Robertson, T. Baxter (c), W. Sorenson,

133

P. Creedy, C. Johnson, D. Blanchard, W. McLennan, G. McDonald, J. Butterfield, A. Atkinson.
France: Dop, Contrastin, Merquey (c), Ducasse, Jiminez, Delpoux, Duplé, Vanel, Audoubert, Fabre, Berthomieu, Montrucolis, Levy.
France T: Merquey 2, Ducasse 2, Vanel; G: Duplé, Montrucolis.
New Zealand T: Moore; G: Moore 3.
Att. 17,914.

10 August France 20 Maoris 28
Huntly
Maoris: : R. Haggie (Auckland), S. George (Waikato), A. Berryman (Waikato), J. Gibbons (Auckland), O. Wright (Auckland), G. Turner (Auckland), J. Wills (Auckland); H. Maxwell (Auckland), J. Tupaea (Waikato), J. Ratima (Auckland), J. Yates (Auckland), A. Hawkes (Auckland), D. Diamond (Auckland).
France T: Savonne 2, Voron 2, Cantoni 2; G: Guilhem.
Maoris T: Berryman 2, Hawkes, Tupaea, Maxwell, George; G: Haggie 5.

13 August France 6 New Zealand 11
Second test: Carlaw Park, Auckland
New Zealand: R. Moore, R. Hawes, R. McKay, B. Robertson, T. Baxter (c), G. Menzies, P. Creedy, W. McLennan, D. Blanchard, C. Johnson, G. McDonald, C. Riddell, A. Atkinson.
France: Dop, Contrastin, Merquey (c), Jiminez, Ducasse, Benausse, Duplé, Vanel, Audoubert, Fabre, Montrucolis, Jammes, Levy.
France T: Contrastin 2.
New Zealand T: Robertson; G: Moore 2, McKay 2.
Att. 14,007.

15 August France 15 Auckland 17
Auckland
France T: Voron, Jiminez, Savonne. G: Benausse 3.
Auckland T: Riddell, Craike, Ratima. G: Haggie 4.
Att. 15,000.

1955 Individual test records in New Zealand

Player	Tests	T	G	Pts.
G. Benausse	1	0	0	0
J. Dop	2	0	0	0
R. Contrastin	2	2	0	6
A. Ducasse	2	2	0	6
J. Merquey	2	2	0	6
A. Jiminez	2	0	0	0
A. Delpoux	1	0	0	0
J. Audoubert	2	0	0	0
J. Vanel	2	1	0	3
J. Fabre	2	0	0	0
G. Berthomieu	1	0	0	0
J. Jammes	1	0	0	0
F. Montrucolis	2	0	1	2
C. Duplé	2	0	1	2
F. Levy	2	0	0	0
Totals:		**7**	**2**	**25**

1960: Third French tour

Australia
14 May	W	France 42 Northern Territory 14 (Darwin)
14 May	W	France 29 Western Australia 8 (Perth)
18 May	W	France 25 Monaro 17 (Canberra)
21 May	W	France 14 Newcastle 10 (Newcastle)
22 May	L	France 23 North Coast 28 (Kempsey)
25 May	W	France 25 Riverina 14 (Wagga Wagga)
28 May	L	France 17 Sydney 23 (Sydney)

29 May	L	France 10 South Division 35 (Wollongong)
1 June	L	France 7 Western Division 14 (Dubbo)
4 June	L	France 7 NSW 25 (Sydney)
11 June	**D**	**France 8 Australia 8 (Sydney)**
13 June	L	France 12 Brisbane 15 (Brisbane)
18 June	L	France 18 Queensland 30 (Brisbane)
19 June	W	France 33 Wide Bay 10 (Maryborough)
22 June	W	France 13 Central Queensland 8 (Rockhampton)
25 June	W	France 26 Far N. Queensland 15 (Cairns)
26 June	W	France 22 North Queensland 5 (Townsville)
2 July	**L**	**France 6 Australia 56 (Brisbane)**
6 July	W	France 33 Ipswich 19 (Ipswich)
9 July	D	France 21 Toowoomba 21 (Toowoomba)
10 July	W	France 24 North Division 10 (Armidale)
16 July	**W**	**France 7 Australia 5 (Sydney)**

Played 22, won 12, drawn 2, lost 8. Points: F: 422, A: 390.

New Zealand

20 July	W	France 32 Waikato 2 (Huntly)
23 July	**L**	**France 2 New Zealand 9 (Auckland)**
25 July	W	France 30 Taranaki 21 (Hawera)
27 July	W	France 41 Wellington 3 (Wellington)
30 July	W	France 15 Canterbury 8 (Christchurch)
31 July	W	France 29 West Coast 5 (Greymouth)
3 August	W	France 23 Maoris 12 (Rotorua)
6 August	**L**	**France 3 New Zealand 9 (Auckland)**
8 August	L	France 5 Auckland 14 (Auckland)

Played 9, won 6, drawn 0, lost 3. Points: F: 180, A: 83.

Overall: Played 31, won 18, drawn 2, lost 11. Points: F: 602, A: 473.

1960 Australian match details

14 May France 42 Northern Territory 14
Gardens Oval, Darwin
Northern Territory: Rouse (c), Boyd, Woolfe, Tanti, Dykes, Thiel, Benny, Hunter, Eckel, Davis, Gerry, Roddy, Flynn.
France: Poletti, Gruppi, Foussat, Jiminez (c), Dubon, Moulinas, Giraud, Rossi, Casas, Boldini, Majoral, A. Lacaze, Marty.
Referee: R. Irvine. Touch judges: N. Letts & R. Spinks.
France T: Foussat 2, Gruppi 2, Giraud, Majoral, Casas, Dubon, Poletti, Moulinas; G: Marty 2, Moulinas 2, A. Lacaze, Dubon.
N. Territory T: Eckel, Davis; G: Rouse 3, Gerry.
Weather: fine/cool. Att. 1,400. (£587).

14 May France 29 Western Australia 8
Belmont Oval, Perth
Western Australia: Hunt, Bassile, Patching, Graffin, Gauci, Taylor, Dickhart, Davies, Kell, Cole, Pascoe, Jones, Morgan.
France: P. Lacaze, Verges, Darricau, G. Benausse, R. Benausse, Mantoulan, Fages, Quaglio, Vadon, Bescos, Mezard, Eramouspé, Barthe.
Referee: D. Coheen. Touch judges: J. Lees & J. Stewart.
France T: Mantoulan 3; G. Benausse, R. Benausse. G: P. Lacaze 7.
W. Australia G: Hunt 4.
Weather: fine. Att. 4,538. (£973).

18 May France 25 Monaro 17
Canberra
Monaro: Bullman, Dawson, Hoy, Blomley, Slavin, Burge, Cameron (c), Maddern, Medway,

135

Patch, Greenwood, Bladen, Sullivan.
France: Poletti, Dubon, Verges, Foussat, Gruppi, Jiminez (c), Giraud, Rossi, Casas, Boldini, Majoral, A. Lacaze, Marty.
Referee: A. Grew. Touch judges: J. McKie & E. Reynolds.
France T: Casas 3, Verges, Rossi; G: A .Lacaze 5.
Monaro T: Bladen 2, Dawson; G: Burge 4.
Weather: windy. Att. 3,000 (£730).

21 May France 14 Newcastle 10
Newcastle Sports Ground
Newcastle: Coleman, Callaghan, Moses, Munro, Adams, Duncan, Giles, Johnson, Williams, Heaney, Owens, Schofield, Gill.
France: P. Lacaze, Foussat, Darricau, G. Benausse, R. Benausse, Mantoulan, Fabre, Bescos, Casas, Quaglio, Mezard, Eramouspé, Barthe.
Referee: J. Jewell. Touch judges: J. Hancock & O. Screen.
France T: G. Benausse 2; G: P. Lacaze 3 + 1 dg.
Newcastle T: Callaghan, Adams; G: Coleman 2.
Weather: fine. Att. 15,096. (£2,708).

22 May France 23 North Coast 28
Kempsey
North Coast: Mason, Jones, Cox, Rankin, Williams, Stanmore (c), McMorrow, Eccleston. McKiernan, Love, Marchment, Golledge, Hampson.
France: Poletti, Gruppi, Jiminez (c) Perducat, Dubon, Moulinas, Giraud, Rossi, Vadon, Boldini, A. Lacaze, Mezard, Marty.
Referee: K. Barwick (Newcastle). Touch judges: M. Livermore & W. Snedden.
France T: Gruppi 2, Dubon, Moulinas, Rossi; G: P. Lacaze 4.
North Coast T: Cox 2, Jones 2, Hampson, Love, Marchment, Williams;
G: Marchment, Williams.
Weather: good. Att. 6,500. (£1,300).

25 May France 25 Riverina 14
Wagga
Riverina: Jones, Robinson, Ratcliff, Honeysett (c), Reardon, Beaven, Sargeant, Kuhn, Negus, Lynch, Crowe, Fowler, Watson.
France: P. Lacaze, Foussat, Jiminez (c), G. Benausse, Gruppi, Mantoulan, Darricau, Quaglio, Casas, Bescos, Eramouspé, Majoral, Barthe.
Referee: A. Grew. Touch judges: L. Lamont & J. Stokes.
France T: Darricau 2, Gruppi, Jiminez, Barthe; G: P. Lacaze 4, Mantoulan 1 (dg).
Riverina T: Beaven, Honeysett; G: Jones 4.
Weather: fine. Att. 11,000. (£1,612).

28 May France 17 Sydney 23
Sydney Cricket Ground
Sydney: Barnes (Balmain) (c), Carlson (Northern Suburbs), Gasnier (St George), Boden (Parramatta), Irvine (Northern Suburbs), Brown (Newtown), Burke (Manly-Warringah), Delamare (Manly-Warringah), Goff (Western Suburbs), Wilson (St George), Brown (Canterbury-Bankstown), Provan (St George), Raper (St George).
France: P. Lacaze, Gruppi, Jiminez (c), G. Benausse, Foussat, Mantoulan, Darricau, Bescos, Vadon, Quaglio, Majoral, Eramouspé, Barthe.
Referee: D. Lawler. Touch judges: W. Devine & E. Tinsley.
France T: Gruppi. G: P. Lacaze 7.
Sydney T: Burke, Raper, Carlson, Irvine, Gasnier. G: Barnes 4.
Weather: fine. Att. 41,808. (£5,755).

29 May France 10 Southern Division 35
Wollongong
Southern Division: Johnston, Kentwell, Hobbs, Fitzpatrick, Horne, Rea, Smith, Olive, Johnson, Maloney, Mulcare, Quinn, Minshall.
France: P. Lacaze, R. Benausse, Dubon, Foussat, Perducat, Moulinas, Giraud, Rossi, Casas, Bescos, Majoral, Mezard, A. Lacaze.
Referee: K. Lyons. Touch judges: A. Grew & T. Jones.
France T: Perducat, Foussat. G: P. Lacaze 2.
Southern Division T: Kentwell 3, Smith 2, Fitzpatrick, Mulcare, Hobbs, Olive. G: Johnston 3, Rea.
Weather: mild. Att. 9,038. (£1,680).

1 June France 7 Western Division 14
Dubbo
Western Division: D. Parish, G. Parish, Weir, Hansen, Scolari, Moore, Lowe, Arrow, Commins, Gilsen, Hambilton, Weldon, Hobby.
France: Poletti, Verges, R. Benausse, Darricau, Perducat, Moulinas, Fages, Rossi, Casas, Quaglio, Majoral, Eramouspé, A. Lacaze.
Referee: R. Curtin. Touch judges: V. Ryan & J. Tink.
France T: Rossi; G: Moulinas 2 (1 dg).
Western Division T: Scolari, Hansen, Hobby, Commins; G: Parish.
Weather: cold and overcast. Att. 5,466. (£1,310).

4 June France 7 New South Wales 25
Sydney Cricket Ground
New South Wales: Barnes (c), Lumsden, Gasnier, Boden, Irvine, Brown, Smith, Delamare, Walsh, Crowe, Lynch, Provan, Raper.
France: P. Lacaze, Gruppi, Jiminez (c), G. Benausse, Perducat, Mantoulan, Fages, Bescos, Casas, Rossi, Majoral, Barthe, A. Lacaze.
Referee: C. Pearce. Touch judges: B. Cowley & J. Martin.
France T: Fages; G: P. Lacaze 2.
NSW T: Lumsden 2, Walsh, Brown, Provan; G: Barnes 5.
Weather: fine. Att. 32,488. (£4,262).

11 June France 8 Australia 8
First test, Sydney Cricket Ground
Australia: K. Barnes(c) (NSW), E. Lumsden (NSW), R. Gasnier (NSW), R. Boden (NSW), K. Irvine (NSW), A. Brown (NSW), B. Muir, G. Parcell (Q), N. Kelly (Q), D. Beattie (Q), J. Paterson (Q), E. Rasmussen (Q), J. Raper (NSW).
France: P. Lacaze, Gruppi, Jiminez (c), G. Benausse, Foussat, Mantoulan, Fabre, Bescos, Casas, Rossi, Eramouspé, Barthe, Fages.
Referee: C. Pearce. Touch judges: A. Konnecke & W. Devine.
France G: P. Lacaze 4.
Australia G: Barnes 4.
Weather: fine. Att. 49,868. (£20,799). KO 2.30pm.

13 June France 12 Brisbane 15
Exhibition Ground
Brisbane: N. Morgan, L. Morgan, Hagan, Haggett, Gray, McCartney, Ryan, Weir, Drennan, Gallagher, McFadden, Veivers, Day.
France: Poletti, Perducat, G. Benausse, Foussat, Gruppi, Jiminez (c), Fages, Vadon, Boldini, Eramouspé, Majoral, Marty.
Referee: J. Purtell. Touch judges: J. Albert & D. Lancashire.
France T: Benausse, Marty. G: Marty 2, Poletti.
Brisbane T: Day. G: L. Morgan 6.
Weather: fine. Att. 17,425. (£2,352). KO 8.00pm (floodlit)

18 June France 18 Queensland 30
Lang Park, Brisbane
Queensland: Drake, L. Morgan, Tait, Weir, Lohman, Banks, Muller, Parcell, Kelly, Beattie, Rasmussen, Paterson, Meehan.
France: P. Lacaze, Gruppi, G. Benausse, Jiminez (c), Foussat, Mantoulan, Fabre, Rossi, Casas, Bescos, Eramouspé, Majoral, Fages.
Referee: J. Casey. Touch judges: J. Purtell & C. Wright.
France T: Bescos, Foussat, Rossi, Gruppi; G: P. Lacaze 3.
Queensland T: Muller 3, Morgan 2, Beattie; G: Lohman 6.
Weather: fine. Att. 22,533. (£5,020).

19 June France 33 Wide Bay 10
Maryborough
Wide Bay: Heidke, Blackman, Little (c), Jackson, Sutton, McKenna, Walsh, Meninga, Melville, Pitts, Grunwald, Wogandt, Eggmollesse.
France: Poletti, Dubon, Perducat, Verges, R. Benausse, Moulinas, Giraud, Quaglio, Vadon, Boldini, Mezard, A. Lacaze, Marty.
Referee: H. Gilbert. Touch judges: N. Coulch & D. Neilsen.
France T: Dubon 2, Verges 2, Perducat, Vadon, Boldini; G: A. Lacaze 6.

Wide Bay T: Blackman, Wogandt; G: Sutton 2.
Weather: fine. Att. 3,982. (£972).

22 June France 13 Central Queensland 8
Rockhampton
Central Queensland: Robinson, Draper, Willie, Leard, Coome, Rycen, Connell, Cridland, Reid, Weeding, Smith, Evans, Ammenhauser.
France: P. Lacaze, Gruppi, Foussat, Jiminez (c), Perducat, Mantoulan, Fabre, Bescos, Vadon, Boldini, Quaglio, Mezard, Eramouspé.
Referee: E. Casey (Townsville). Touch judges: C. Jackson & A. Volling.
France T: Gruppi 2, Eramouspé; G: P. Lacaze 2.
Central Queensland T: Cridland, Connell; G: Robinson.
Weather: rain. Att. 4,000. (£928). KO 8.00pm.

25 June France 26 Far North Queensland 15
Cairns
Far North Queensland: Gill, Brunkle, Jenkins, Shipp, Dent, Miller, Firth, Allendorf, Thompson, Coyne, McKenzie, Crema, Ryan.
France: Poletti, Verges, Jiminez, A. Lacaze, Barthe, Darricau, Giraud, Majoral, Casas, Rossi, Boldini, Fages, Marty.
Referee: W. Gayler. Touch judges: F. Faithful & A. Stanley.
France T: Verges 3, Poletti, A. Lacaze, Jiminez; G: A. Lacaze 4.
Far North Queensland T: Miller, Brunkle, Firth; G: Brunkle 2, Allendorf.
Weather: good. Att. 4,329. (£1,271).

26 June France 22 North Queensland 5
Townsville
North Queensland: Snelling, Hendry, Warnick, Hester, Potts, Cook, Aili, Campbell, Paterson, Eaton, Beecheno, Clifford, Meehan.
France: P. Lacaze, Gruppi, Perducat, Dubon, Foussat, Mantoulan, Fabre, Quaglio, Vadon, Bescos, Eramouspé, A. Lacaze, Mezard.
Referee: W. Gayler (Ipswich). Touch judges: J. Power & E. Casey.
France T: Foussat, Gruppi, Mezard, Mantoulan; G: P. Lacaze 4, Mantoulan.
N. Queensland T: Potts; G: Hendry.
Weather: fine. Att. 5,457. (£1,927).

2 July France 6 Australia 56
Second test: Brisbane
Australia: K. Barnes (NSW) (c), L. Morgan (Q), R. Gasnier (NSW), H. Wells (NSW), K. Irvine (NSW), R. Banks (Q), R. Bugden (NSW), E. Rasmussen (Q), W. Rayner (NSW), R. Mossop (NSW), B. Hambly (NSW), N. Provan (NSW), J. Raper (all NSW).
France: P. Lacaze, Gruppi, Jiminez (c), Foussat, Dubon, Mantoulan, Fabre, Bescos, Vadon, Quaglio, Eramouspé, Barthe, Fages.
Referee: D. Lawler. Touch judges: W. Gayler & R. Massey.
France G: P. Lacaze 3.
Australia T: Bugden 3, Irvine 3, Morgan 2, Provan 2, Gasnier, Hambly; G: Barnes 10.
Weather: showers. Att. 32,644. (£16,553). KO 3.00pm.

6 July France 33 Ipswich 19
Ipswich
Ipswich: Malone, McDonald, Gwynne, Lindsay, Pegg, Barrett (c), Brown, Beattie, Christison, Parcell, Cleary, Scully, Bell.
France: Poletti, Verges, A. Lacaze, Perducat, Darricau, Moulinas, Giraud (c), Boldini, Casas, Rossi, Majoral, Mezard, Marty.
Referee: D. Lancashire. Touch judges: W. Gayler & R. Diflo.
France T: Verges 2, Poletti, Majoral, Marty, Mezard, Giraud; G: A. Lacaze 6.
Ipswich T: Barrett, Scully, Gwynne; G: Barrett 5.
Weather: fine. Att. 2,704. (£481).

9 July France 21 Toowoomba 21
Toowoomba
Toowoomba: Drake, Lohman, Fitzgerald, Gil, Marks, Gleeson, Muller, Rasmussen (c), Holmes, Cook, Morris, Duncan.
France: P. Lacaze, Dubon, Jiminez, Perducat, Gruppi, Mantoulan, Darricau, Quaglio, Vadon, Bescos, Eramouspé, Barthe, A. Lacaze.

Referee: C. Wright. Touch judges: C. Gray & L. Toleman.
France T: Gruppi 2, Giraud 2, Bescos; G: P. Lacaze 3.
Toowoomba T: Lohman 2, Drake, Gleeson, Cook; G: Lohman 3.
Weather: fine. Att. 9,818. (£2,811).

10 July France 24 Northern Division 10
Armidale
Northern Division: Koch, Ritchie, Lingwood, Gilligan, Smith, Apps, Solway, Cooke, Hardman, Brown, Mitchell, Killen, Rodgers.
France: Poletti, Verges, Perducat, Mantoulan, Dubon, Moulinas, Darricau, Rossi, Casas, Boldini, Majoral, Mezard, Marty.
Referee: N. Spohr. Touch judges: G. McCarter & N. Brown.
France T: Perducat 2, Darricau, Marty, Boldini, Rossi. G: Mantoulan 3.
Northern Division T: Solway, Hardman. G: Rodgers 2.
Weather: rainy. Att. 6,200. (£1,378).

16 July France 7 Australia 5
Third test: Sydney Cricket Ground
Australia: K. Barnes (NSW) (c), K. Irvine (NSW), R. Gasnier (NSW), H. Wells (NSW), L. Morgan (Q), R. Boden (NSW), R. Bugden (NSW), R. Mossop (NSW), W. Rayner (NSW), E. Rasmussen (Q), B. Hambly (NSW), N. Provan (NSW), J. Raper (NSW).
France: Poletti, Dubon, Fabre, Mantoulan, Marty, Jiminez, Giraud, Bescos, Vadon, Boldini, Quaglio, Eramouspé, Barthe.
Referee: D. Lawler. Touch judges: B. Cowley & J. O'Connor.
France T: Dubon; G: Mantoulan 2.
Australia T: Bugden; G: Barnes.
Weather: fine. Att. 29,127. (£11,658). KO 2.30 pm.

1960 Individual playing records in Australia

Player	Tests	Others	T	G	Pts.
P. Lacaze	2	10	0	49	98
L. Poletti	1	8	3	1	11
J. Dubon	2	8	5	1	17
J. Foussat	2	10	5	0	15
R. Gruppi	2	11	12	0	36
R. Benausse	0	5	1	0	3
J. Verges	0	7	8	0	24
A. Perducat	0	11	4	0	12
G. Benausse	1	7	4	1	14
C. Mantoulan	3	10	4	6	24
J. Darricau	0	9	3	0	9
A. Jiminez	3	11	2	0	6
R. Moulinas	0	7	2	4	14
B. Fabre	3	4	0	0	0
J. Giraud	1	7	4	0	12
A. Quaglio	2	9	0	0	0
M. Bescos	3	10	2	0	6
A. Boldini	1	9	2	0	6
F. Rossi	1	10	5	0	15
A. Casas	1	11	4	0	12
A. Vadon	2	8	1	0	3
J. Barthe	3	7	1	0	3
R. Eramouspé	3	10	1	0	3
Y. Mezard	0	9	2	0	6
R. Majoral	0	12	2	0	6
A. Lacaze	0	11	1	22	47
G. Fages	2	6	1	0	3
A. Marty	1	8	3	4	17
Totals			**82**	**88**	**422**

1960 New Zealand match details

20 July France 32 Waikato 2
Huntly
Waikato: O. Hinton, G. Caywood, R. Tait, R. Spiers, A. Berryman, B. Porteous, G. Farrar, A. Lindop, R. Shearan, D. Dow, N. Smith, D. Solomon, B. Barakat.
France: Poletti, G. Benausse, Fabre, Mantoulan, Perducat, Jiminez, Giraud, Bescos, Vadon, Boldini, Barthe, Eramouspé, Marty.
France T: Marty 2, Giraud 2, Benausse, C. Mantoulan, Fabre, Poletti; G: Giraud 4.
Waikato G: Berryman.
Att. 3,071

23 July France 2 New Zealand 9
First test: Auckland
New Zealand: C. Eastlake, B. Hadfield, G. Turner, R. Griffiths, N. Denton, G. Menzies, N. Roberts, C. Johnson (c), J. Butterfield, H. Maxwell, T. Kilkelly, R. Ackland, M. Cooke.
France: Poletti, Dubon, Fabre, Mantoulan, Perducat, Jiminez (c), Giraud, Boldini, Vadon, Bescos, Eramouspé, Quaglio, Barthe.
France G: Giraud.
New Zealand T: Hadfield 2, Denton.
Att. 17,914

25 July France 30 Taranaki 21
Hawera
Taranaki: B. Lambert, J. Chapman, S. Sturmey, B. Christianson, R. Southern, C. Murray, P. Moller, J. Broughton, G. O'Carroll, M. Casperson, R. Bertrand, K. Peters, M. Woods.
France: P. Lacaze, Verges, Darricau, Foussat, Gruppi, Moulinas, Fages, Rossi, Casas, Boldini, Mezard, Majoral, A. Lacaze.
France T: Foussat 3, Moulinas, Fages, Verges; G: P. Lacaze 6.
Taranaki T: Bertrand, Moller, Southern, Casperson, Broughton; G: Lambert, Southern 2.
Att. 1,234

27 July France 41 Wellington 3
Wellington
Wellington: W. Harrison, C. Tarawhiti, S. McDonald, J. Dodd, R. Andrews, P. Fox, B. Ewart, A. Still, L. Pilcher, T. Poona, M. Beri, P. Gregory, H. Winchman.
France: Poletti, Dubon, Fabre, Mantoulan, Perducat, Jiminez, Giraud, Quaglio, Vadon, Bescos, Eramouspé, Barthe, Marty.
France T: Dubon 4, Perducat, 2, Mantoulan, Bescos, Quaglio; G: Giraud 7.
Wellington T: Still.
Att. 1,701

30 July France 15 Canterbury 8
Christchurch
Canterbury: A. Smith, A. Amer, R. Turton, J. Bond, K. Harding, P. Smith, K. Roberts (c), F. Tinning, N. Diggs, K. Pearce, M. Mohi, J. Fisher, M. Cooke.
France: P. Lacaze, R. Benausse, Gruppi, Foussat, Verges, Darricau, Fages (c), Quaglio, Vadon, Bescos, Mezard, Majoral, A. Lacaze.
France T: Darricau, Fages, Foussat; G: P. Lacaze 3.
Canterbury G: Smith 4.
Att. 7,529.

31 July France 29 West Coast 5
Greymouth
France T: Barthe 2, Poletti 2, Mantoulan, Perducat, Fabre; G: Giraud 4.
West Coast T: Butterfield; G: Kennedy.
Att.4,500.

3 August France 23 Maoris 12
Rotorua
Maoris: J. Radonovich (Auckland), T. Katene (Bay of Plenty), A. Berryman (Waikato), J. Pirihi (Auckland), H. Walters, (Auckland), W. Snowden (Auckland), W. Kem (Auckland), S. Edwards (Bay of Plenty), E. Cooke (Auckland), H. Baker (Auckland), J. Matthews (Auckland), P. Gregory (Wellington), W. Hattaway (Auckland).

France: P. Lacaze, Dubon, Verges, Gruppi, R. Benausse, Moulinas, Darricau, Rossi, Casas, Majoral, A. Lacaze, Mezard, Fages (c).
Referee: H. Hobman (Auckland)
France T: A. Lacaze 2, Dubon, Moulinas, Rossi; G: P. Lacaze 4.
Maoris T: Baker, Berryman; G: Katene 3.
Att. 5,044.

6 August France 3 New Zealand 9
Auckland
New Zealand: C. Eastlake, B. Hadfield, G. Turner, R. Griffiths, N. Denton, G. Menzies, N. Roberts, C. Johnson (c), J. Butterfield, H. Maxwell, K. Kilkelly, R. Ackland, M. Cooke.
France: Poletti, Foussat, Jiminez (c), Mantoulan, Perducat, Fabre, Giraud, Bescos, Vadon, Boldini, Quaglio, Eramouspé, Barthe.
France T: Foussat.
New Zealand T: Hadfield; G: Eastlake 3.
Att.14,007

8 August France 5 Auckland 14
Auckland
Auckland: Fagan, Denton, Turner, Sorenson, Hadfield, Eastlake, Snowden, Johnson, Patterson, Maxwell, Riddell, Ackland, McKay.
France T: Mezard; G: P. Lacaze.
Auckland T: Fagan, Denton, Sorenson, Riddell; G: Sorenson.
Att. 11,431.

1960 Individual test records in New Zealand

Player	Tests	T	G	Pts.
L. Poletti	2	0	0	0
J. Dubon	1	0	0	0
J. Foussat	1	1	0	3
A. Perducat	2	0	0	0
C. Mantoulan	2	0	0	0
A. Jiminez	2	0	0	0
B. Fabre	2	0	0	0
J. Giraud	2	0	1	2
A. Quaglio	2	0	0	0
M. Bescos	2	0	0	0
A. Boldini	2	0	0	0
A. Vadon	2	0	0	0
J. Barthe	2	0	0	0
R. Eramouspé	2	0	0	0
Totals:		**1**	**1**	**5**

Rugby League books from
London League Publications Ltd

Fascinating study on the early floodlit matches of the 1870s. Also includes modern developments, including the 1955 ITV Trophy and the BBC2 Floodlit Trophy.

Published in July 2007 at £11.95

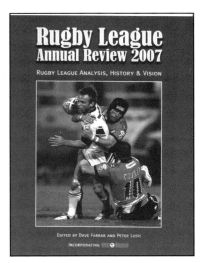

New annual published in February 2007, including promotion & relegation, Amateurism: The case for an 'open' game, Rugby league and the media, Wembley and the Challenge Cup, Mike Gregory Warrington's new stadium Ireland, Wales, Scotland and London, Aussie Rules and rugby league, St Helens Recs St Helens and Mal Meninga Rugby league and World War One, book reviews and obituaries.

Published April 2007 at £12.95.

Order from any bookshop, or from www.llpshop.co.uk (credit card orders), or by cheque from London League Publications Ltd, PO Box 10441, London E14 8WR. All orders post free.